1/2020

CRAZY CONTRAPTIONS

BUILD RUBE GOLDBERG MACHINES THAT SWOOP, SPIN, STACK, AND SWIVEL

WITH HANDS-ON ENGINEERING ACTIVITIES

LAURA PERDEW

ILLUSTRATED BY MICAH RAUCH

More engineering titles in the **Build It Yourself** series.

Check out more titles at www.nomadpress.net

Nomad Press

A division of Nomad Communications

10 9 8 7 6 5 4 3 2 1

This book was manufactured by Versa Press, East Peoria, Illinois
October 2019, Job #J19-06340
ISBN Softcover: 978-1-61930-826-8
ISBN Hardcover: 978-1-61930-823-7

Educational Consultant, Marla Conn

Questions regarding the ordering of this book should be addressed to
Nomad Press
2456 Christian St., White River Junction, VT 05001
www.nomadpress.net

Printed in the United States.

CONTENTS

Interested in Primary Sources? Look for this icon.

Use a smartphone or tablet app to scan the QR code and explore more! Photos are also primary sources because a photograph takes a picture at the moment something happens. You can find a list of URLs on the Resources page. If the QR code doesn't work, try searching the internet with the Keyword Prompts to find other helpful sources.

🔎 Rube Goldberg

About 2.5 million . . . . During the Stone Age, early
years ago   humans use wedges made
                                   of stone as a cutting tool.

About 200,000 . . . . . . Early humans begin to
years ago   use levers as tools.

3500 BCE . . . . People in Mesopotamia first use the
                                   wheel and axle as a pottery wheel.

Circa 3000 BCE . . . . . . First known use of the chariot.

Circa 2500 BCE . . . . . . The Egyptians begin building the
                                   pyramids using inclined planes.

Circa 1500 BCE . . . . . . The Mesopotamians use a
                                   pulley system to lift water.

Seventh century BCE . . Mesopotamians use large screws as
                                   a tool to raise water for irrigation.

Third century BCE . . . . Archimedes discovers how levers
                                   work. He also explains the
                                   mechanical advantage of pulleys.

Fifteenth century CE . . The printing press is invented
                                   using a screw press.

Seventeenth century . . Sir Isaac Newton develops the
                                   laws of gravity and later presents
                                   his three laws of motion.

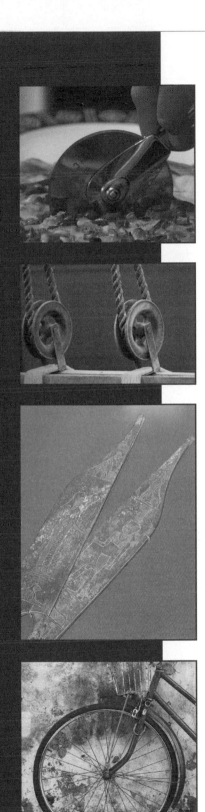

1743 . . . . The first known elevator for humans, which uses a pulley system, is installed in the Palace of Versailles in France for King Louis XV.

1858 . . . . John Landis Mason designs a screw-on lid to secure lids onto jars used for canning fruits and vegetables.

July 4, 1883 . . . . Rube Goldberg is born in California.

1903 . . . . Mary Anderson patents windshield wipers, which are a type of lever.

1949 . . . . The first Rube Goldberg machine contest is held at Purdue University in Indiana.

1968 . . . . The Mattel toy company launches the first Hot Wheels toy cars.

December 7, 1970 . . . . Rube Goldberg dies, leaving behind a legacy of humor and "inventions" that serve as inspiration for engineering crazy contraptions.

1988 . . . . The Rube Goldberg machine contest is revived with the assistance of the Goldberg family, and becomes an annual event.

1995 . . . . A U.S. stamp is issued featuring the Self-Operating Napkin cartoon in honor of Rube Goldberg.

MEET RUBE
GOLDBERG

Have you ever watched a line of dominoes fall? Have you ever played the game *Mouse Trap*? Do you like to think of complex ways to accomplish simple tasks?

You might love doing **Rube Goldberg**–like projects without even knowing what they're called! This is what we call activities that involve creating a series of chain reactions to perform a specific task. And not just any kind of task: one that would be far easier to simply do with your two hands, but which ends up being a lot of fun when you design an entire machine around the task.

Sound crazy? Let's meet the man who started this craze!

1

WORDS TO KNOW

engineer: someone who uses math, science, and creativity to solve problems and build things.

contraption: a newfangled or complicated **device**.

device: a piece of equipment meant to do certain things, such as a phone.

chain reaction: a series of events in which one action causes the next one and so on.

convoluted: complex and difficult to follow.

pulley: a simple machine consisting of a wheel with a **grooved** rim that a rope or chain is pulled through to help lift up a load.

groove: a line cut into a surface, often made in order to guide something such as rope along the rim of a wheel in a pulley system.

simple machine: a tool that uses one movement to complete work.

catapult: a device used to hurl or launch something.

MEET RUBE

More than a hundred years ago, a man named Reuben Lucius Goldberg (1883–1970) was born on July 4, 1883, in San Francisco, California. Who knew this child would have a profound effect on the way millions of people thought about engineering? Who knew he would grow up to make so many people laugh and wonder?

Early on, Rube was interested in art. By age eight, his interest had turned into a passion. Rube loved creating line drawings and tracing pictures from newspapers and magazines. Rube's father wasn't too keen on his son's interest in art, though. So, when Rube grew up, he went to college to become an **engineer**. He graduated from UC Berkeley in 1904 with an engineering degree. Afterward, he worked for the City of San Francisco's Water and Sewer Department designing pipe systems.

Rube Goldberg with his wife and children in 1929. Members of Goldberg's family still run his estate.

After only six months, he quit. Instead, Rube Goldberg started working for a San Francisco newspaper. While he was there, he submitted cartoons and drawings to the newspaper's editorial staff, hoping to get published. But Goldberg often discovered his cartoons in the editor's trash bin!

Then, one day, he was given the chance to sketch athletes for the sports section. The newspaper staff soon discovered they sold more papers when there were more pictures. Why do you think this was?

Once the paper began running a color cartoon section, Goldberg finally had a place for his cartoons. His career had begun. Eventually, he moved across the country to New York City, New York. That's where his work as a cartoonist became even more popular and he became famous.

Goldberg was a great cartoonist, but he became a household name because of the elaborate, overly complicated, hilarious, crazy **contraptions** he drew. These contraptions were extremely complicated **chain reactions** that, in the end, performed very simple tasks. Some of his wacky contraptions include an automatic back-scratcher, an alarm clock, a self-opening umbrella, a "simplified" pencil sharpener, and a fly swatter. He also created an orange squeezer for fresh orange juice in the morning and even had an elaborate plan for pulling an olive out of a jar.

The contraptions Rube Goldberg invented were funny not only because they were so **convoluted**, but because they often included unusual parts. He used animals in the designs. He also used springs, **pulleys** and other **simple machines**, rockets, feathers, melting ice, escalators, fire, **catapults**, and more.

This short video will give you a quick introduction to the world of Rube Goldberg machines. Have you ever built a Rube Goldberg machine before? Did it meet your objective?

🔍 Rube Goldberg legacy Vimeo

CRAZY CONTRAPTIONS

One of his most famous contraptions was a self-operating napkin. That cartoon involved a catapulting cracker, a parrot, a lighter, a launching sky-rocket, a sickle, and a pendulum with a napkin attached that swung back and forth across a diner's face. The artist even recommended

Rube Goldberg drew about 50,000 CARTOONS during his lifetime.

replacing the napkin with a harmonica after dinner for a little music! His contraptions were absurd. And people loved them.

What would Goldberg think of next? His drawings of contraptions were so popular that Rube Goldberg is now an adjective in the dictionary!

Self-Operating Napkin by Rube Goldberg

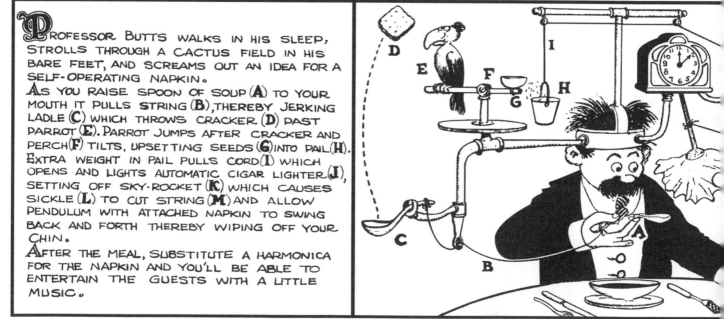

PROFESSOR BUTTS WALKS IN HIS SLEEP, STROLLS THROUGH A CACTUS FIELD IN HIS BARE FEET, AND SCREAMS OUT AN IDEA FOR A SELF-OPERATING NAPKIN.
AS YOU RAISE SPOON OF SOUP (**A**) TO YOUR MOUTH IT PULLS STRING (**B**), THEREBY JERKING LADLE (**C**) WHICH THROWS CRACKER (**D**) PAST PARROT (**E**). PARROT JUMPS AFTER CRACKER AND PERCH (**F**) TILTS, UPSETTING SEEDS (**G**) INTO PAIL (**H**). EXTRA WEIGHT IN PAIL PULLS CORD (**I**) WHICH OPENS AND LIGHTS AUTOMATIC CIGAR LIGHTER (**J**), SETTING OFF SKY-ROCKET (**K**) WHICH CAUSES SICKLE (**L**) TO CUT STRING (**M**) AND ALLOW PENDULUM WITH ATTACHED NAPKIN TO SWING BACK AND FORTH THEREBY WIPING OFF YOUR CHIN.
AFTER THE MEAL, SUBSTITUTE A HARMONICA FOR THE NAPKIN AND YOU'LL BE ABLE TO ENTERTAIN THE GUESTS WITH A LITTLE MUSIC.

ENGINEERING AT WORK (AND PLAY!)

Interestingly, Rube Goldberg did not actually build any of the contraptions he drew. However, his mechanical mind is evident in his work. Each machine he created used real engineering concepts and was designed to actually work, even though he really drew them to simply make people laugh.

Take a look at one of Rube Goldberg's invention drawings. You will see that there are letters used as labels in the drawing. Beside the drawing, there is a written description of the chain reaction. Each letter shows an **energy** transfer. Energy transfers can take many, many different forms in **physics**.

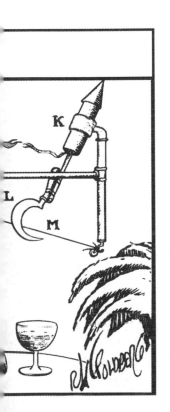

In Rube Goldberg's machines, it means the movement of energy from one part of the chain reaction to the next. The main principle here is that once the everyday objects in his drawings were set in motion, the energy would be transferred throughout the invention to ultimately perform a simple task.

Rube Goldberg Inc.

Rube Goldberg died in 1970, yet his name and **legacy** live on. Not only do Rube Goldberg's "inventions" still make people laugh, but today, Rube Goldberg Inc. is a nonprofit company that promotes **STEM** and STEAM education for kids of all ages. It holds annual contests for kids ages eight and older. And it hosts an online gallery where visitors can enjoy much of Goldberg's work.

There are traveling exhibitions of the art of Rube Goldberg and a children's exhibit called the World of Hilarious Inventions. Rube Goldberg Inc. has educational materials to bring the enjoyment of engineering Rube Goldberg contraptions into classrooms and homes everywhere.

If you want a closer look at Goldberg's work, visit the gallery on the Rube Goldberg Inc. website. What surprises you about these pictures?

🔎 Rube Goldberg image

PS

WORDS TO KNOW

force: a push or pull applied to an object that changes an object's motion.

gravity: a force that pulls objects toward each other and all objects to the earth.

lever: a simple machine made of a rigid bar that **pivots** on a support, called a fulcrum.

pivot: to turn or move on a fixed spot.

technology: the tools, methods, and systems used to solve a problem or do work.

Goldberg also employed his knowledge of **force** and **gravity** to keep things moving. We'll take a closer look at those in the next chapter!

Another important aspect of Rube Goldberg's machines is the use of simple machines. Each of these machines interact with one another to keep the chain reaction going. For example, in the Self-Operating Napkin contraption, the ladle that throws the cracker to the parrot is a **lever**. And the string holding the small pail of seeds is on a pulley system. As you become an expert on Rube Goldberg contraptions, you'll be able to spot the simple machines in his drawings and use them in your own contraptions!

His contraptions poked fun at people's obsession with new **technology** at the time. Engineers design practical machines to make life easier. The simplest designs are the best—and the fewer parts, the more reliable the machine will be. Rube Goldberg machines were anything but simple!

Kids testing their Rube Goldberg machine

Credit: U.S. Army photo by Merv Brokke, AMRDEC

Take the Challenge!

Even though Rube Goldberg never built any of the machines he designed, he was an inspiration to engineers young and old. In 1949, two college students at Purdue University started a contest to see who could build the best Rube Goldberg machine. The contest was held every year until 1955. In 1988, the first official live Rube Goldberg machine contest took place with the support of the Goldberg family.

That first contest was for college students. Several years later, in 1996, the contest was opened to a second age group, 14 to 18. Now there are also divisions for students ages 11 to 14 and 8 to 11.

The annual contest features a new task each year. Past tasks have included toasting a slice of bread, assembling a hamburger, and applying a bandage. The contest encourages entrants to find inspiration in Rube Goldberg machines to create their own machines that "accomplish a simple task in the most complicated—and funniest—way possible." The contest requires creative problem solving, science, teamwork . . . and a sense of humor.

The annual student competitions sponsored by Rube Goldberg Inc. are both live and online. **You can check out some of the past winners here.**

🔍 Goldberg contest

NOW IT'S YOUR TURN

Do you like to take things apart to see how they work? Do you like to build things? Do you have ideas for inventions? Do you like a creative challenge? Then you should try building crazy contraptions!

The supplies listed in this book are only suggestions. Try to find your own supplies. Dive into a pile of junk! Raid the recycling! Scavenge through old toy chests! Keep your eyes open—you never know when or where you might come across something that will be perfect for a crazy contraption. Oh yes, you will also need graph paper and an old notebook or journal when designing your contraptions.

Next, consider what problems you want to solve. What simple task will your contraption perform? There are suggestions for those in the back of the book, too. But, use your imagination and you'll probably come up with a bunch more that aren't listed.

The absolute, **MOST IMPORTANT**, can't-build-without thing you will need when creating Rube Goldberg contraptions is **YOUR IMAGINATION**.

Each chapter of this book contains many challenges. They start small and get bigger. Don't try to create some huge, wacky contraption right away. Start small and let your contraptions grow as you gain experience. Every challenge in this book includes drawings of contraptions to give you a place to start. But if you have a better idea for a contraption, go for it!

A gigantic Rube Goldberg machine, inspired by the board game *Mouse Trap*!
Credit: Bill Ward (CC BY 2.0)

A couple of things before you get started. First, this might get messy. Be ready to clean up the mess you will undoubtedly create. Remember to ask permission to do anything that might seem out of the ordinary or to use anything that is not yours.

Also, keep in mind that sometimes, your contraptions will fail. Not to worry! When your contraption doesn't work, like all good engineers, you must ask the big question, "Why?" Asking questions and figuring out what went wrong is part of the engineering design process.

Essential Questions

Each chapter of this book begins with an essential question to help guide your exploration of engineering and building crazy contraptions. Keep the question in your mind as you read the chapter. At the end of each chapter, use your notebook to record your thoughts and answers.

ESSENTIAL QUESTION

What was Rube Goldberg's contribution to engineering?

Building contraptions can be frustrating, and you may even need to ask for help or bring in a partner. Teamwork puts lots of minds together, which is another thing engineers do. Finally, engineering crazy contraptions should be enjoyable. See how absurd you can be. Use your creativity. Laugh. Make your contraptions more and more complicated. And above all else . . . have FUN!

Engineering Design Process

Every engineer keeps a notebook to keep track of their ideas and their steps in the engineering design process. As you read through this book and do the activities, keep track of your observations, data, and designs in a design worksheet, like the one shown here. When doing an activity, remember that there is no right answer or right way to approach a project. Be creative and have fun!

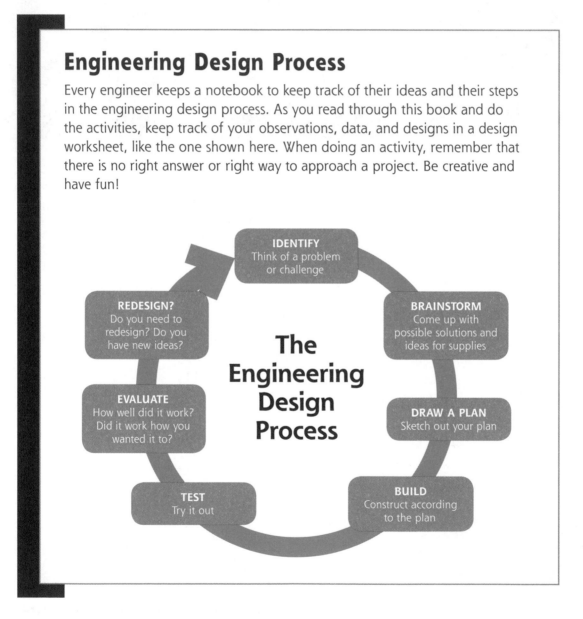

DRAW YOUR OWN
CARTOON

Time to get started! One thing engineers and designers do a lot of is drawing. You might think they dive right in with materials, but no—they dive right in with pencils and paper. Start your creative juices flowing by drawing your own cartoon, just like Rube Goldberg.

❯ **Open your Rube Goldberg notebook.** Page one will be your table of contents, so turn to page two. Label the page number on the bottom. At the top, title the page with the name of the challenge and the date.

❯ **Now, consider chores in your own everyday life that you don't like doing.** Feeding the dog? Washing the dishes? Taking out the trash? Imagine if you could design a contraption that would do that simple task for you!

❯ **This first challenge is for you to draw your own Rube Goldberg-esque cartoon** that will accomplish that simple task in a humorous and complicated way. Because you are only sketching, and not building, this machine, you can use really crazy stuff in it, such as alligators and rockets and fire! Put all that stuff in your drawing now because when it gets to actually making contraptions, you won't be using those kinds of things. We don't want anyone getting eaten by alligators.

❯ **Remember to label each part of the chain reaction with a letter.** Then, write a description of each step below the drawing. You might not know much about engineering crazy contraptions yet, but let Rube Goldberg's work be your inspiration. See what you can come up with.

Try This!

Don't worry if your drawing skills aren't perfect . . . use stick figures! What's important is following the action of the contraption and being as creative as possible.

Chapter 1

THINGS YOU SHOULD KNOW BEFORE YOU
GET STARTED

There are a few things to know before you start building contraptions. You will learn a lot about creating Rube Goldberg machines on your own by using the engineering design process discussed in the introduction and designing, building, experimenting, testing, evaluating, and rebuilding.

But before you dive in, let's talk about how our world works. Let's talk about the way that objects move.

As you read this chapter, use a ball to do activities that will help you understand complex concepts. Why does it help to see a concept acted out? Because that lets you learn with your mind, eyes, and hands!

ESSENTIAL QUESTION

What roles do force, work, and energy play in Rube Goldberg contraptions?

FIRST LAW OF MOTION

Long before Rube Goldberg's time, there was a man named Sir Isaac Newton (1643–1727). This guy with the fancy name and funny hair developed the laws of motion in the 1600s. There are three of them, and they all describe specific ways that every object moves every time it moves. Let's start with the first!

An object in motion will stay in motion (moving in the same direction at the same speed) unless some force acts on it. And, an object at rest will stay at rest unless some force acts on it.

The **first law of motion** might seem strange—objects don't just keep moving forever and ever. Do they? Can you imagine what it would be like if they did? The key part of Newton's first law is "unless some force acts on it." That's why objects stop.

Let's test the idea. Have that ball? Bounce, throw, or kick it (you probably want to go outside to do this). The reason it will eventually stop moving is because a force acts on it (details on that later).

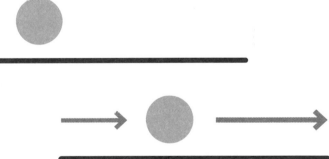

Remember, a force is a push or a pull applied to an object that changes an object's motion. If nothing had interfered, your ball would still be in motion. Now, is that ball you bounced just sitting there? It will stay in that place (resting) unless you (or something else) interacts with it to get it moving again. It will not start moving all by itself.

WORDS TO KNOW

second law of motion: a push or a pull on an object will change the speed of motion. The heavier an object is, the more force is needed to make that object speed up or slow down.

mass: the measure of how much **matter** is in an object; the weight of an object in relation to its size.

matter: anything that has weight and takes up space. Almost everything is made of matter!

physicist: a scientist who studies physics.

knighted: given the title "Sir" by a British king or queen in recognition of one's achievements or service to his country.

Why does all this matter, you ask? Because when you are building contraptions, you will need to get things moving somehow. And, you will need to figure out how to keep them moving, because there will be forces out there getting in your way.

SECOND LAW OF MOTION

Let's move on to Newton's **second law of motion**. It explains that how fast an object speeds up depends on the **mass** of the object and the force applied to it.

Sir Isaac Newton

Sir Isaac Newton was born in the mid-1600s in England. He went to school for a while, where he was an okay student. Then, his mother took him out of school to become a farmer. Isaac wanted none of that and went back to school. Eventually, he grew up to be a **physicist**, astronomer, and a mathematician, and one of the most important people in the scientific revolution of the seventeenth century. His best-known work was called the *Philosophiae Naturalis Principia Mathematica* (which means *Mathematical Principals of Natural Philosophy*). It was in this book that he described the laws of motion. It was also here that he defined the laws of gravity. He made many other key contributions to science. Because of this, he was **knighted** in 1705. That's why we call him "Sir."

Portrait of Sir Isaac Newton
credit: Godfrey Kneller, 1702

A push or a pull on an object will change the speed of motion. The heavier an object is, the more force is needed to make that object speed up or slow down.

Give your ball a push. As it's rolling, give it another push. By doing this, you are changing the speed of the ball. If you give it a small push, it will only go so far. However, if you apply more force with a harder push, the ball will speed up and go farther.

In other words, the
HARDER YOU PUSH,
bounce, throw, or kick your ball,
the **FASTER AND FARTHER IT WILL TRAVEL**.

The other part of Newton's second law of motion is that objects with more mass are harder to get moving and harder to slow down. Imagine you have a kickball and a bowling ball. The bowling ball has A LOT more mass than the kickball and will need more force to get it moving. Therefore, rolling a kickball is WAY easier than rolling a bowling ball. And don't even try kicking a bowling ball!

Even athletes use physics! Watch this video about a seemingly impossible free kick made by Roberto Carlos of Brazil in 1997. Physics explains why this kick was possible. It also explains how precisely he had to kick the ball to make it happen.

🔎 TED-Ed football physics

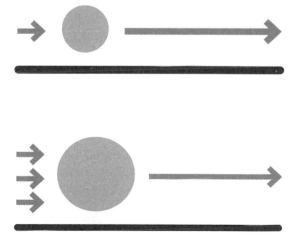

Of course, these laws of motion don't apply just to that ball you're playing with. They apply to everything. So, when you are building your contraption, you'll want to consider how to get the different objects in it to speed up or slow down. You may also need to figure out how to apply more force to get something moving faster.

THIRD LAW OF MOTION

Newton's **third law of motion** states that for every action, there is an equal and opposite reaction. Forces always occur in pairs—an action force and a reaction force. Both forces are the same size but move in opposite directions.

For every action, there is an equal and opposite reaction.

Picture yourself going up to bat in a baseball or softball game. When the ball hits the bat, the ball **exerts** an action force on the bat. At the same time, the bat exerts a reaction force on the ball. Sometimes, you can feel this force in your arms.

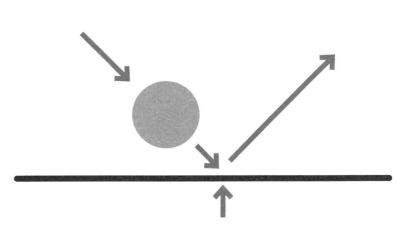

The same is true for the ball you've been using. Let's say you kick it across your yard. When you kick it, you exert an action force on the ball. The ball also exerts an equal and opposite reaction force on your foot. This happens when the ball bounces, too. It will hit the ground and bounce in the opposite direction from which it landed.

It's important to remember the three laws of motion as you build contraptions, because when you create an action force, you need to think about what the reaction will be. You don't want contraption parts flying off in all directions! Even if this does happen, don't give up. Your contraption building will require lots of trial and error. And that's okay. We can learn a lot from our mistakes.

FORCES

Let's talk a little more about forces. A force is defined as a push or pull on an object. That's it. The push or pull will cause an object to stay in one place, speed up, slow down, change shape, or even change direction. When you bounced, threw, or kicked that ball, you applied force to the ball.

FORCES are measured in units called **NEWTONS,** named after **SIR ISAAC NEWTON.**

Forces are all around you and come in many shapes and sizes. Probably the biggest force in our lives is gravity, which pulls objects toward the ground. That ball you've been using always falls to the ground, doesn't it? That's gravity!

Albert Einstein's Idea About Gravity

A couple hundred years after Sir Isaac Newton defined the law of gravity, Albert Einstein came along and shook things up. He said that what we perceive as the force of gravity isn't really that at all. He explained that the force we perceive actually has to do with the curve of space and time caused by a mass. And that warped time and space is what is responsible for keeping objects on the ground on Earth. This is called the theory of general relativity. **Take a look at this video to learn more!**

space.com
general relativity

WORDS TO KNOW

legend: an old story usually based on historical facts but that is not proven to be true.

orbit: the path of an object circling another object in space.

friction: the force that slows a moving object or objects when they move against each other.

potential energy: the stored energy of an object due to its state or position.

kinetic energy: the energy of an object in motion.

In addition to the laws of motion, Sir Isaac Newton was also responsible for defining the laws of gravity. There is a **legend** that says that he began to contemplate gravity when he saw an apple fall from tree. Some even say that he was under the tree and the apple hit him on the head!

No matter how it happened, Newton began to wonder about the force that caused the apple to fall. He also wondered if that same force kept the planets in **orbit**. His observations led him to explain the movement of the sun and the planets, as well as how gravity works on Earth.

The **GRAVITATIONAL PULL** of the sun and moon are responsible for the **TIDES** of Earth's oceans!

Friction is another type of force. Friction occurs when two objects move against each other. When your ball was flying through the air, the air molecules actually slowed it down. That's why it didn't fly along forever!

An easier way to see friction in action is to roll your ball over a smooth, hard surface, such as a floor or countertop. Now take your ball and try to roll it on carpet or grass. Can you tell the difference? It is much easier to roll the ball across the smooth surface—because there's less friction. That's also why the grass on sports fields is cut short. And remember that bowling ball? Bowling alleys are smooth, so the balls roll easily down the lanes.

You will apply forces when you make contraptions. The trick will be applying enough force in the right place to keep the chain reaction going and to keep objects in motion in the direction you want.

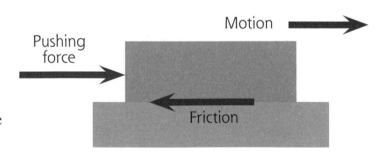

WORK AND ENERGY

All that bouncing, throwing, or kicking a ball you've been doing is work. Remember, work is when a force acts on an object to move it some distance. However, reading this book is not considered work. What? Nope. Reading is not work—according to scientists, anyway.

For something to qualify as work, you have to exert a force AND move something. In science, work is defined as a force acting on an object in order to move that object some distance. When you push or pull an object, creating a force, and that object moves, work is being done. That means throwing or kicking your ball around is work!

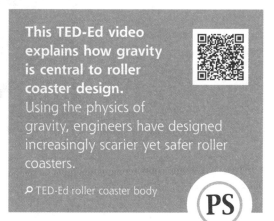

This TED-Ed video explains how gravity is central to roller coaster design. Using the physics of gravity, engineers have designed increasingly scarier yet safer roller coasters.

℘ TED-Ed roller coaster body

In order for work to happen, though, there must be energy. Think about how you feel. If you don't have a lot of energy, you can't do much work. But, if you have eaten well and slept well, you have more energy and can do more work.

The same is true for everything—energy is needed in order to move things. This energy comes in two forms—**potential energy** and **kinetic energy**. Potential energy is energy waiting to happen, which is stored in an object. If you are sitting on your bike at the top of the hill, the bicycle has potential energy (and you are about to have a great ride!) because of its position. The same is true for a marble sitting at the top of a marble run in a Rube Goldberg contraption.

A stretched-out
RUBBER BAND
is another example of
POTENTIAL ENERGY.

WORDS TO KNOW

inclined plane: a flat surface with one end raised higher than the other.

wheel and axle: a wheel with a rod that turn together to lift and move loads.

axle: the rod around which a wheel **rotates**.

rotate: to turn around a fixed point.

wedge: a simple machine that is thick at one end and narrows to a thin edge at the other. A wedge is used for splitting, tightening, and securing objects.

screw: a simple machine that has an inclined plane wrapped around a central **axis**. It is used to lift objects or hold things together.

axis: the center, around which something rotates.

nut: a donut-shaped piece of metal with screw **threads** on the inner circle. Used with a bolt through the center to hold things together.

threads: the inclined plane that wraps around the axis of the screw.

bolt: a metal pin with screw threads. Used with a nut around the outside of the pin to hold things together.

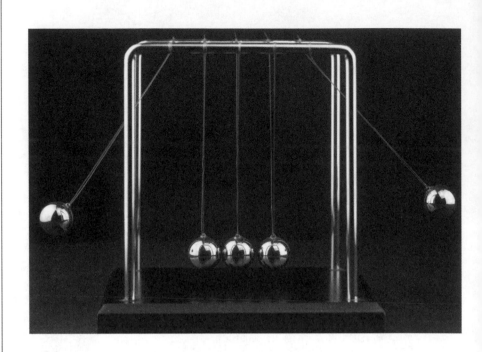

Which marbles have kinetic energy?
Which have potential energy?

credit: Sheila Sund (CC BY 2.0)

Kinetic energy is energy in action. Once you kick off on that bicycle headed downhill, the bicycle has kinetic energy. The marble rolling down the marble run has kinetic energy.

When Rube Goldberg invented his machines, he continually transferred energy from one object to the next. Remember, each of those energy transfers was marked by a letter. Go look at the cartoon on page 4. Now that you know about energy, you can better understand the energy transfers.

If you were to **SNAP** that rubber **BAND**, that's more energy in action— **KINETIC ENERGY**.

When you build your own contraptions, you will need to keep the same principles in mind. In order to do the work of keeping the parts of the contraption in motion, you must have energy to apply a force.

SIMPLE MACHINES

Throughout history, in order to do work, people created machines to help. The six simple machines include **inclined planes**, levers, **wheels and axles**, pulleys, **wedges**, and **screws**. Each of these tools does one or more of the following: increase the strength of a force, change the direction of a force, or change the distance over which you apply a force needed to do work.

As you learn more about each of these simple machines, you will see how they can be used to design and **BUILD YOUR CRAZY CONTRAPTIONS**. Not only that, you'll learn how to combine them to **ENGINEER** contraptions that are more complicated and **FUN!**

Where Are the Simple Machines?

Each of these simple machines are, well, simple! They have very few, if any, moving parts. And they are very much a part of your everyday life. Take a look at where you will find some of these simple machines!

› **Inclined planes:** ramp, slide, stairs

› **Levers:** crowbar, seesaw, light switch

› **Wheels and axles:** car, revolving door, fan

› **Pulleys:** window shade, flagpole, elevator

› **Wedges:** pizza cutter, doorstop, nail

› **Screws:** jar lid, **nuts** and **bolts**

You'll learn lots more about these simple machines in the coming chapters.

While simple machines make the work easier, the amount of work accomplished is the same. In other words, the same work gets done, but you have to put in less effort. This is the **mechanical advantage** you gain by using a simple machine.

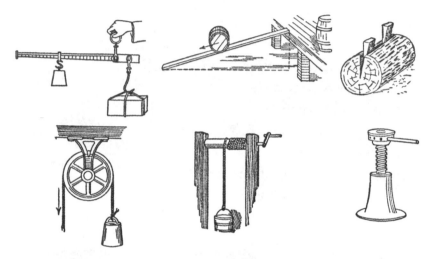

Simple machines in use throughout history. Do you recognize any?

Remember, an engineer is someone who designs and builds structures, systems, and machines. That's going to be you! Look back in the Introduction for more about the engineering design process, and use it for all of your building projects.

This video shows the engineering design process in action. Professional engineers discuss how they apply this process to designing and constructing real buildings.

🔎 PBS engineering design

ESSENTIAL QUESTION

What roles do force, work, and energy play in Rube Goldberg contraptions?

BALLOONS AND THE
LAWS OF MOTION

It's time to see for yourself how the laws of motion work. When you inflate a balloon, you are filling it with air that is under pressure. When that air is released, it creates a force on the balloon. This experiment will help you understand the forces at work and how different variables affect the movement of the balloon.

❯ **Begin by threading the string through a straw.** Then, attach the string to two anchor points that are 10 to 15 feet apart and 3 to 5 feet off the ground. Make sure the string is tight.

❯ **Blow up the balloon about halfway, but don't tie it off** (use large bag clips or binder clips to keep the air from escaping).

❯ **Carefully tape the balloon to the straw on the string.** Pull the balloon back to an anchor point so that the open end of the balloon is closest to the anchor point.

❯ **Let go! Measure and record how far the balloon travels.** How was the balloon's movement an example of Newton's third law of motion?

❯ **Now, test Newton's second law.** How fast and far the balloon goes depends on how much force is acting on it AND the mass of the balloon. Start by adding more force than before by blowing up the balloon even more. Does it travel even farther? Measure and record how far it goes.

❯ **Finally, blow up the balloon only a little bit** and record how far it goes. Measure and record how far it traveled.

❯ **Compare the distance the balloon traveled** in each of the three trials. What have you discovered about force and the second law of motion?

❯ **To add mass to your balloon, tape objects to it** (coins, popsicle sticks, paper clips). Now, test how far the balloon travels with different masses. What do you discover?

Try This!

Redo this challenge, trying more variations of mass and force. Use a stopwatch to time how fast the balloon gets from one point to another under different circumstances. Can you find a combination that gets the balloon to travel longer than you thought possible?

NEWTON SUPPORTS
SEAT BELTS

If Sir Isaac Newton was around now, he would certainly be in favor of seat belts in cars. In fact, he'd use his first law of motion to explain why.

❭ **To understand his point of view, create a small cart** with low sides that can travel down a tabletop ramp. You can use a toy car and attach a shallow basket or cup to the top or make your own.

❭ **Use a stack of books to prop up one end of a ramp.** At the bottom of the ramp, create a barrier that will stop the cart. Your barrier is going to create a force!

❭ **Put a marble in the cart at the top of the ramp.** Now, let go. What happened to the marble when the cart stopped abruptly at the bottom of the ramp? How is this an example of Newton's first law of motion?

Try This!

Use Newton's first law of motion and your experiment to justify why you think seat belts are important. Write a newspaper article explaining why you (and Newton) support the use of seat belts in cars.

Engineering Careers

While engineering crazy contraptions may just be for fun, engineering itself is a serious profession. There are many types of engineers who work in many different fields to design and build structures, systems, and machines that help people. One of the most well-known types of engineer is a civil engineer. They are the people responsible for designing and constructing buildings, roads, bridges, and dams. Mechanical engineers create power-producing systems. We also have electrical, aerospace, computer, and software engineers. There are even environmental engineers who work to protect and improve the environment. Engineers influence all aspects of life!

Chapter 2

PLAY WITH
INCLINED PLANES

Time to do some work AND have fun! The first simple machine you will use is an inclined plane. An inclined plane is just the term for a flat surface with one end higher than another. That's it. Simple.

Inclined planes are very useful simple machines because they help us raise or lower things gradually. Think about walking up a ramp or hiking trail versus climbing a cliff edge. It is easier to use the ramp or trail (the inclined plane) than it is to go straight up.

ESSENTIAL QUESTION

How do inclined planes help people do work and build Rube Goldberg contraptions?

No one actually invented the inclined plane—**planes** exist in nature. Before the physics of inclined planes was truly understood, people were using them as an engineering tool to make life (and work!) easier.

WORDS TO KNOW

plane: a flat or level surface.

aqueduct: a pipe, channel, canal, or bridge built to carry water.

Mesopotamia: an ancient civilization located between the Tigris and Euphrates Rivers, in what is today part of Iraq.

slope: a plane with one end higher than the other.

perpendicular: a line at a 90-degree angle, called a right angle, to another line, plane, or surface.

grade: in physics, the amount of slope on an inclined plane.

efficient: work done with little waste of time or energy.

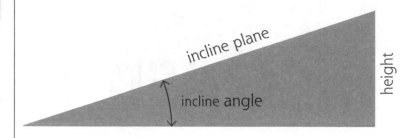

Egyptians had this figured out thousands of years ago when they built the pyramids. They used inclined planes to push the huge stones UP the pyramids. Building the pyramids at that time would not have been possible without inclined planes.

Other ancient civilizations built **aqueducts** to carry water DOWN into city centers from far-off places. Some of the earliest aqueducts were built on Crete and in **Mesopotamia**. The ancient Greeks also had water systems that included aqueducts. But it was the Romans, known for being master engineers, who constructed vast networks of pipes, channels, and bridges to bring water to Rome.

Check out this PBS video that explains how the Egyptian pyramids were built with precision more than 4,000 years ago, despite not having any modern tools or technology.

🔎 PBS pyramid science 2

PS

They built the network to have a regular **slope** and allowed gravity to do the work of carrying water. This was much easier than fetching it by hand!

Inclined planes are all around us. The slide at the park is an inclined plane. So is a roller coaster, a ramp, a road with a slope, and pipes. Ladders and stairs are inclined planes, too, because they are slanted, not **perpendicular** to the ground.

The largest of the three Egyptian **PYRAMIDS** of Giza is approximately 480 feet tall. It was built entirely by hand out of more than **2 MILLION** massive blocks of stone.

Grand Central Terminal

In the early 1900s, it became clear that New York City needed to upgrade its railyard and train station. In addition to replacing the steam locomotives with electric trains, the railroad's president recommended building an entirely new station. The new building became what is today known as Grand Central Terminal. When it was built, it was the first station that had no stairs. Instead, it had ramps. The designers knew that instead of just moving objects, the ramps would help move people. They tested many different slopes and finally settled on a **grade** that would accommodate everyone, from older travelers and small children to people toting luggage and those in wheelchairs. The design proved **efficient** at moving the flow of people through the station swiftly. Today, New York's terminal is still regarded as one of the grandest in the world.

credit: Diliff (CC BY 2.5)

WORDS TO KNOW

angle: the figure formed when two lines meet at the same point.

brainstorm: to think creatively and without judgment, often in a group of people.

Look around your home or neighborhood for other examples of inclined planes. Do you have stairs in your home or apartment? Ramps at your school? See how many examples of inclined planes you can find.

HOW INCLINED PLANES HELP

Inclined planes make moving things up (or down) easier because they give you a mechanical advantage, like all simple machines. What this means is that if you use an inclined plane, you will need less force to move an object.

When you use an inclined plane to **MOVE AN OBJECT**, you will need to move it a **GREATER DISTANCE** to get it to its destination.

If you make the plane less steep by reducing the **angle**, but longer, you gain even more of a mechanical advantage. That's because the inclined plane spreads the work out across a greater distance. In the end, though, the amount of work stays the same. So you pick! You can put in a lot of force for a short distance or less force for a longer distance.

One of the most famous buildings that uses inclined planes as part of the design is the Guggenheim Museum in New York. The building was designed by the architect Frank Lloyd Wright. **Take a look at the museum in this video.**

🔎 Guggenheim plan visit

Let's say you and several friends are building an epic snowman. You've rolled a large body as the base. Together, you've managed to get the middle snowball on. But now that the head is rolled and ready to mount, you discover that the last snowball is too heavy and the snowman is now too high to get the head on the snowman.

You could give up and settle for a two-snowball snowman. Or, you **brainstorm**! How could you get it up there? How about with an inclined plane? By rolling the snowball up the inclined plane to place it on top of the snowman, you've gained a mechanical advantage. And you now have a really large, really cool snowman to show off your physics knowledge.

The bed of a **DUMP TRUCK** is an inclined plane when one end is raised to empty a load. It is much **EASIER TO TILT** the bed of a dump truck to empty it than to move the contents out by hand.

We've discussed moving objects UP using an inclined plane. And you know that the steeper the plane, the harder it is to climb or move something up it. The same principles

apply if you use an inclined plane to move something down. If you are moving something down a ramp, the steeper the ramp, the faster the object will go.

Think about slides at the park. The one for little kids isn't usually as steep or as long as the one for bigger kids. That's so little ones don't end up going too fast.

When building your crazy contraptions, you will use inclined planes A LOT. What do you already have in your home that you could use as an inclined plane?

Wheelchair Ramps

While inclined planes themselves have been used by humans for thousands of years, ramps for wheelchairs have become standard in buildings and on streets only in the last few decades. For people with disabilities, ramps are a necessity that allow many wheelchair users to move independently. Even a curb on a sidewalk can pose a daunting and risky challenge to someone in a wheelchair. But it wasn't until 1990 that people with disabilities were protected under the law in the United States. The American Disabilities Act (ADA) assured that people with disabilities had the same rights and access to public places as everyone else. Among other things, the law holds that public buildings must have accommodations for people in wheelchairs, which includes ramps. Sidewalks today are also built with ramps at the curbs. Ramps are now increasingly incorporated into the built environment as a part of the design.

Any flat surface is a plane if you tilt one end up. For example, tilting up one end of a book turns it into an inclined plane. Pieces of cardboard boxes make good inclined planes, too. Same for pieces of wood. Toy car tracks and train tracks would also make great inclined planes.

Getting stuck on what you can use for an inclined plane? Remember, there's also a list of everyday items on page 118 that you can turn to for help.

PLAYGROUND SLIDES date back to at least the early 1900s, maybe earlier. Since the first wood and metal slides, they have changed through time and taken many forms, including longer and **HIGHER** slides, **TUNNEL** slides, **WATER** slides, and **SPIRAL SLIDES**.

ESSENTIAL QUESTION

How do inclined planes help people do work and build Rube Goldberg contraptions?

KNOCK IT
OVER

This is your first contraption challenge. Ready?

Use the engineering design process for this challenge and all the challenges in the book. The step-by-step process will walk you through making, testing, and evaluating your contraptions. The first step is to identify a problem. In the case of Rube Goldberg contraptions, you are deciding what simple (and ridiculous) task you want to build a machine for. Each contraption challenge has identified a task for you to complete, but if you have better ideas, go for it!

The Challenge Identified: Use an inclined plane and something that can roll or slide down the plane to knock over an object. Yes, this is a ridiculous little task! That's what crazy contraptions are all about.

> **Brainstorm ideas and supplies:** What will you use for your inclined plane? Cardboard? A book? A notebook? What moving object will you use on the inclined plane (a ball, a marble, a toy car, etc.)? Also think about what you want to knock over. A Lego guy? A small stuffed animal? Maybe you want your moving object to knock a ball off the table. You decide.

> **Draw a plan:** Your plan might look something like this (but then again, it might look totally different!)

random ball

book
(inclined plane)

other
books

one armed
Lego dude

Testing the Plane

Set up an inclined plane on a smooth surface, not carpet or grass. Raise one end about an inch off the ground using books or blocks. Place an object at the top of the plane and let go. What happens? Raise the top end of the inclined plane another couple of inches and try again. Do this several more times, with higher heights. What do you discover? Why didn't your object keep moving across the surface at the bottom of the plane forever? What forces got in the way? Which laws of motion are at play in this experiment? How will you apply what you've learned here to your Rube Goldberg contraptions?

> **Build:** Okay, so the term "build" might be a bit of a stretch. It's more like: incline your plane!

> **Test:** Release your object and let it roll down the plane.

Contraption Hint: Empty toilet paper and paper towel tubes make GREAT inclined planes. They also make excellent building materials!

> **Evaluate:** Were you able to knock over your object? If not, you need more force. You might need to raise the plane a little bit so the slope is steeper and the object you are rolling down the plane will roll faster. Another problem you might have encountered was that the rolling item missed its target. What materials could you use that would help keep your moving object on a straight path?

> **Redesign?** You may need to incline your plane more. You might want to use other moving objects to slide or roll down the plane. Or, you may want to find other things to knock over. Then, try it all again.

PYRAMID
DEMOLITION

Let's make things a little more complicated. Now you will use two or more inclined planes together.

The Challenge Identified: Use *two* inclined planes (or maybe you want to try *three*!) and something that can roll or slide down the ramps to knock over a pyramid you build.

▶ **Brainstorm ideas and supplies:** Your two planes can use the same materials or they can use different materials. Consider how you will raise one plane above the other. You will also need to figure out what you want to build your pyramid out of and what moving object you will use.

▶ **Draw a plan:** There are a couple ways to think about the challenge. Your two planes could keep the moving object headed downward in the same direction.

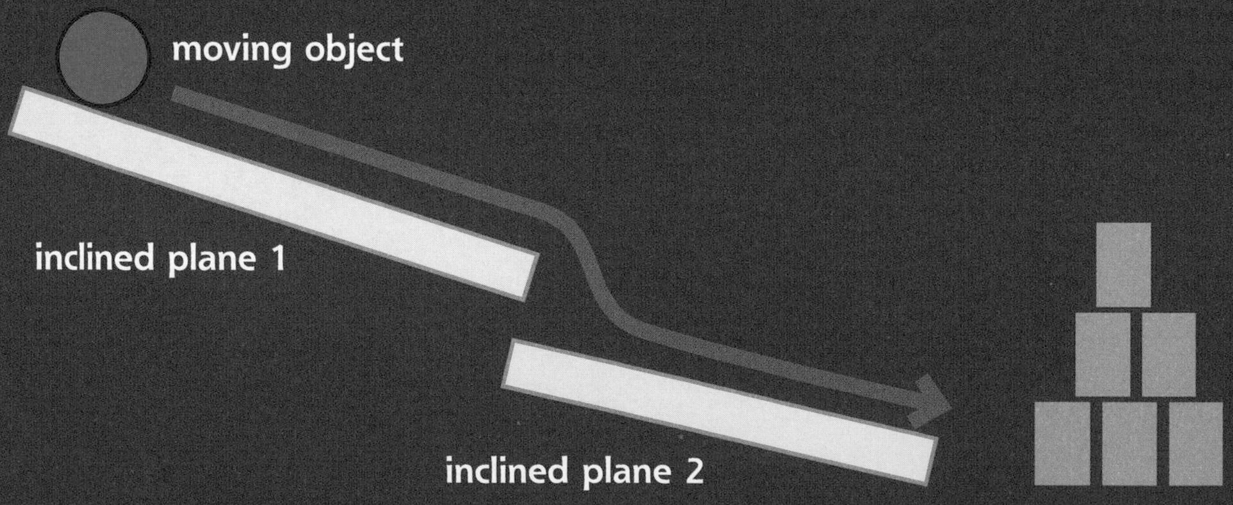

moving object

inclined plane 1

inclined plane 2

❯ Or, the second plane could make the moving object change direction.

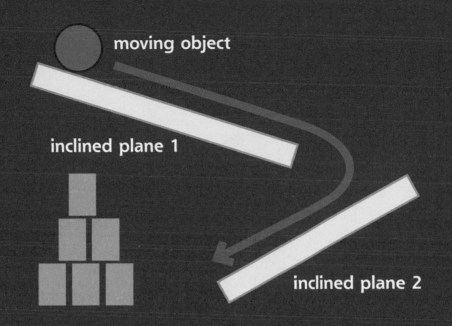

moving object

inclined plane 1

inclined plane 2

❯ **Build:** Putting this contraption together is going to take a little more time because you will need to figure out how to raise the first plane above the second.

❯ **Test:** Go ahead—send the object down the inclined plane.

❯ **Evaluate:** How did your two planes function together? Did the moving object miss the second plane? Maybe you want to use a different moving object. Or, maybe you need to line up the two planes more carefully or stabilize them more. Was there enough force to knock down the pyramid you built? If not, you may need to incline your planes more. Or maybe you need a moving object with greater mass.

❯ **Redesign?** How could you redesign this mini-contraption? Could you use different materials? Move things around? Add elements?

SUPER CHALLENGE

How many inclined planes can you use in a single simple contraption? As you add on inclined planes, try to use different objects as the plane. Also, try using different objects to move down the planes—marbles, cars, trains, Ping-Pong balls, and more. Can you figure out how to get an object to move up an inclined plane?

Chapter 3

LOOKING AT
LEVERS

Now that you know about inclined planes, it's time to make those contraptions just a little bit more complicated—and more fun. Adding more elements to a contraption increases the chances it won't work on the first try, but part of the satisfaction of building a contraption is sticking with it until it does work. One way to make your inventions more complex is to add a lever or two. Or three!

A lever is simply a bar or plank, called an **arm**, which sits on a fixed point, called a **fulcrum**. The lever moves on that point. Every lever has both an arm and a fulcrum.

Think about you and a friend sitting on either end of a seesaw—which is a lever. The plank of the seesaw moves on the fulcrum in the middle. Where are the forces applied when you go up and down?

ESSENTIAL QUESTION

What role do levers play in today's world?

TIME FOR CLASS!

There are different kinds of levers. Some, like the seesaw, have the fixed point in the middle. The **load** is on one end and the force is applied at the other. These are called **first class levers**. As you push DOWN on one end of the lever, the load on the other side of the fulcrum goes UP. In this case, the direction of the force changes.

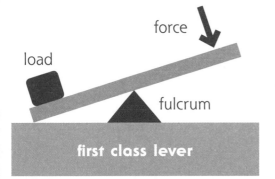

force

load

fulcrum

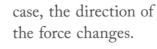

first class lever

Second class levers have the fulcrum at one end. The load is in the middle and the force is applied at the other end. As with the first class lever, the second class lever changes the amount of force you need to apply to move an object by spreading the work out over a distance.

With second class levers, though, the direction of the force does not change. A wheelbarrow is one example. The load goes in the middle and you pick up the handles of the wheelbarrow to move the load. When you do this, both the force you apply and the load move upwards.

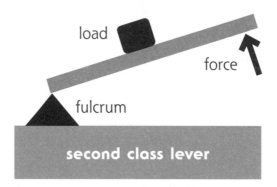

second class lever

Finally, some levers have the fulcrum at one end, the load on the other end, and the force is applied in the middle. These are called **third class levers**. As with second class levers, the direction of the force does not change—but the amount and distance across which the force is applied do change.

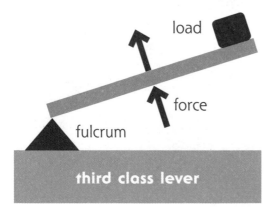

third class lever

A fishing rod is a great example of a **THIRD CLASS LEVER**.

LEVERS EVERYWHERE

Watch this TED-Ed video to learn more about the math and science behind the lever and the relationship between the force applied and the distance to the fulcrum.

🔎 TED-Ed mathematics lever

Now that you know about levers, you might be able to spot them all around you. For example, did you know that a car's windshield wipers are actually levers?

There is an old saying that goes, "Necessity is the mother of invention." This means that most things are invented because someone sees a need. Such was the case with windshield wipers. In 1902, Mary Anderson (1866–1953) was on a trolley while visiting New York City. It was a cold, snowy day.

During her ride, Mary observed that the driver had to put his head out the side window in order to see. He even stopped the trolley many times to clean the windshield by hand. She began to brainstorm how the windshield could be kept clear mechanically.

Back at home in Alabama, Mary Anderson drew many sketches and conducted many experiments. Her final idea became the world's first

windshield wiper. It consisted of a hand-operated lever inside the vehicle. The lever triggered a spring-loaded arm (another lever!) attached to a rubber blade. There was also a **counterweight** to make sure the wiper stayed in contact with the windshield.

WORDS TO KNOW

primates: a group of intelligent animals that includes humans, apes, and monkeys.

patent: a legal document that gives an inventor the sole right to their invention so that others may not make, use, or sell the invention.

balance scale: a device used for weighing things that balances weight on one side of the lever with what's being weighed on the other side.

irrigation: a system for bringing water through ditches to farmland.

BCE: put after a date, BCE stands for Before Common Era and counts down to zero. CE stands for Common Era and counts up from zero. These non-religious terms correspond to BC and AD. This book was printed in 2019 CE.

Even **ANIMALS USE LEVERS**. Have you ever seen a **SEA OTTER** use a rock to pry open a seashell? They are using the rock as a lever! **BIRDS** have also been observed using levers. **Primates** use sticks as levers, too, and for many other tasks as well!

Mary received a **patent** for her invention in 1903. However, the growing automobile industry was not at all interested in her invention at that time. It was only several decades later that automobile companies made windshield wipers standard equipment. Luckily, Mary lived long enough to see her invention become an important part of every car made.

There is evidence that people have been using levers for more than 200,000 years. The simplest levers were tools used to open fruit and shells. Later, people used levers to launch spears and lift water. Levers were also used in **balance scales**. Other levers included oars on boats and hoes for farming. Using levers allows people to do a lot of easy work instead of a little bit of hard work. And some of that hard work might not even get done without a lever!

Just as with inclined planes, levers are all around you. The claw of a hammer acts as a lever when you pull out nails. Scissors and tweezers are examples of two levers working together.

When you play baseball, you are using a lever—the bat! Brooms, rakes, and hoes are levers, too. You can even find levers on your own body—take a look at your arms and legs!

This advertisement by Samsung has quite a few different types of levers in it. **See how many you can pick out as you watch.**

🔎 2D house Samsung Goldberg

PS

Even though levers are everywhere, they might not be as easy to spot as inclined planes. Walk around your home. Look in a tool box or a toy bin. Can you find five more examples of levers?

HOW LEVERS HELP

The Shaduf

A shaduf is an example of a first class lever, first used in ancient Egypt to raise water for **irrigation**. A shaduf consists of a long lever or pole on a wood frame, with a bucket attached to one end and a counterweight on the other. To use it, the bucket is lowered into a canal or river and filled with water. Then, the bucket of water is raised by pushing down on the counterweight. Using the lever makes raising water much easier for farmers. It is still used in parts of the world today.

Levers help us move, launch, and lift loads by reducing the amount of force needed to do the work. Think about trying to remove a nail stuck in a piece of wood. Most likely you wouldn't be able to pull it out with your fingers, unless you had superhuman strength. But, if you use the claw of a hammer, you can probably get it out. This is because, as with all other simple machines, the lever gives us a mechanical advantage.

Levers don't reduce the amount of work needed to move or lift an object, but they do reduce the amount of force needed because it is applied over a greater distance. Therefore, as with the inclined plane, the longer the lever, the greater the mechanical advantage.

The first person to truly study and describe the mathematical principles of the lever was Archimedes (288–212 **BCE**), an ancient Greek mathematician. His study of the lever (and also the pulley and the screw) in the third century BCE really added to our knowledge of how things work.

credit: Lance Cpl. Robert D. Williams Jr.

Knowing what he did about the principles of the lever, he claimed, "Give me a place to stand, and I shall move the earth." While in reality, he'd never be able to find a lever long enough, nor would he be able to find a place to stand in outer space, Archimedes's claim still illustrates his understanding of how the lever works.

Think of you and your friend on the seesaw again. If you both weigh the same, you teeter back and forth easily. But what happens if your older brother gets on the other end? Or your dad? The teetering gets a lot harder! You can still do it if you move back on the seat to spread out the work you need to do to lift your heavier seesaw partner. You are using your weight as the force. Lifting your partner is the work. The seesaw is the lever.

Levers are an important part of making crazy contraptions. You can use them to move, launch, or lift different objects. There are probably many things in your home that would make a good lever. Some ideas include a ruler, popsicle sticks, or even pencils. Toys such as Lincoln Logs, Legos, or Tinker Toys can be used as levers, too. Even a book can be used as a lever. Go see what you can find!

Now that you've got some knowledge about levers, you can use it to make some crazy contraptions!

While this video is an advertisement created by Sprice Machines, the chain reaction in it has many, many levers. As you watch, remember that seesaws and dominoes are levers. How many can you count in this small machine?

🔎 Sprice Fatherly

PS

Hinges

Imagine that every time you wanted to open a door you had to pick it up and move it aside. Not fun, right? But with a second class lever, it's easy! The oldest known hinges date back to 1600 BCE, to the city of Hattusa, the capital of the ancient Hittite Empire. Later, the ancient Egyptians, Babylonians, and Assyrians used hinges in public buildings. The ancient Romans began to use hinges in the home for doors and cabinets as well as in armor to make it more flexible! During the 1600s, hinges were brought to the Americas with the colonists. Today, hinges are used around the world. Your home probably has dozens of hinges of various sizes and shapes.

ESSENTIAL QUESTION

What role do levers play in today's world?

COLLAPSING
CARDS

For your first lever challenge, perform a simple task using one type of lever—a domino. Dominoes act as third class levers when you set them on end. The end on the table is the fulcrum. The domino itself is the arm, and when it falls, it applies force to the middle of next domino.

The Challenge Identified: Build a simple contraption made of dominoes to destroy a house of cards.

> **Brainstorm ideas and supplies:** Well, you'll need dominoes and playing cards. What happens if you don't have these supplies? What else could be used like a domino? Could you make your own cards cut out of cereal boxes?

> **Draw a plan:** This is a pretty simple challenge. Your drawing might look something like this one.

> **Build:** Set up your house of cards. Steady hands! Stand your dominoes on end in a line, making sure the last one is close enough to the card house to knock into it when it falls.

> **Test:** Ready? Knock over that first domino. Watch the chain reaction of one lever (a domino) falling into the other.

> **Evaluate:** Did the dominoes fall like you expected? Did your house of cards fall? What went well? If the cards didn't fall, you need more force. Try moving the last domino closer to the house. You might also add larger, heavier dominoes to the chain.

> **Redesign?** You may want to add more dominoes (LOTS more!). You could even experiment with making the line of dominoes snake across a table. You could also set up the chain reaction to make the falling dominoes move in two different directions. Or perhaps you could make your house of cards even bigger!

Contraption Hint: Several old cereal boxes, CD cases, books, or even wooden blocks make great dominoes if you don't have actual dominoes.

TREAT
LAUNCHER

Catapults are another type of lever. The part of the catapult that does the launching is the arm, and the point where the catapult is attached is the fulcrum. Once you've made this catapult, you'll be able to use it again in later challenges.

The Challenge Identified: Create a catapult that will toss a treat to your dog (or cat or hamster or little sister). If you don't have any of those, you can create a marshmallow launcher!

▶ **Brainstorm ideas and supplies:** Your catapult frame can be made of anything—popsicle sticks, pencils, straws, boxes, cans, tubes, etc. Or, do you have any toys that could be used to make the frame of a catapult? Plastic spoons make a good launching arm, but surely you can think of other items if you don't have a plastic spoon. You will need rubber bands or elastic hairbands also.

▶ **Draw a plan:** There are many types of catapults, from very simple to large and complex. How complicated do you want your catapult to be?

Your plan might look like this: OR it might look totally different, like this:

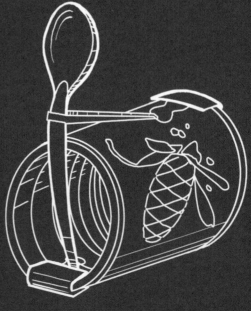

Catapult 1   Catapult 2

How to Make a Catapult

There are a lot of ways to make a simple catapult, and you don't need any fancy supplies. The internet can help you find a design using materials you already have. Try one of these websites.

little bins popsicle catapult

diy marshmallow catapult

frugal fun catapult

Build: This will take a little time, plus some trial and error. But remember, failing is okay! Learn from your mistakes and try again.

> **Test:** Find your dog and a treat. Time for launch!

> **Evaluate:** Did your catapult launch the treat the way you expected it to? Was the launch better than you expected? Worse? What parts might you need to fiddle with? How much did the dog like this challenge?

> **Redesign?** You may need to improve the catapult's launch. You might want to increase the launch distance or the accuracy. Or, you may want to make a completely new catapult out of different materials.

WORDS TO KNOW

trial and error: trying first one thing, then another and another, until something works.

RING
A BELL

Are you ready to move on and make a bigger contraption? Combine what you've learned about levers and inclined planes to make something completely new!

The Challenge Identified: Create a contraption that uses both a lever and an inclined plane to ring a bell.

Brainstorm ideas and supplies: You could use either of the levers from the other challenges. Or, you could make a new one. Maybe a seesaw? Also consider what you will use for the inclined plane or planes. Perhaps you still have the materials you used in the previous chapter. Obviously, you need a bell (and if you don't have one, **improvise!**).

Contraption Hint: If you want to make a seesaw for your contraption, a ruler (the arm) with a TP roll attached at the middle (the fulcrum) is easy to put together. You might also use some kind of plank or piece of cardboard as the arm, with a Lincoln Log in the middle as fulcrum. A large binder clip can serve as a fulcrum, too.

▶ **Draw a plan:** Sketch out how your inclined plane and lever will function together. There are lots of possibilities.

▶ **Build:** Assemble your contraption.

WORDS TO KNOW

improvise: to create with little preparation using materials easily obtained.

Test: Start the chain reaction and ring that bell!

Evaluate: Did the bell ring? Could it ring louder? Longer? How did your planes and your levers perform together? How might you move things around for a better result? Did your contraption apply too much force or do you need more to get the bell to ring?

Redesign? Do you need to redesign your contraption? During the build, did you come up with other ideas about how to ring the bell? Or, maybe you just want to add a few elements to make the contraption more complicated. You could also find a different type of bell.

SUPER CHALLENGE

Create a contraption that uses three or more different types of levers. Perhaps this would include dominoes, a catapult, and a seesaw. Or, maybe you have even better ideas! Can you use five different types of levers in a contraption?

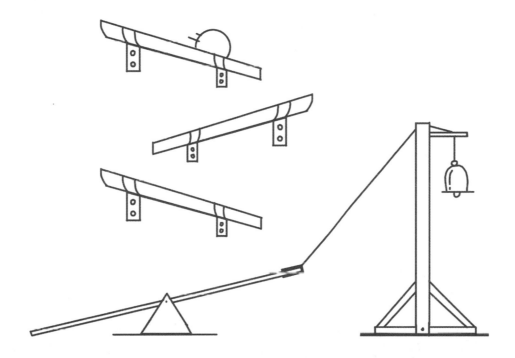

Chapter 4

WHOA! WHEELS AND AXLES

Now that you've got your head around a couple of different simple machines, let's get things rolling even more and look at a third simple machine, the wheel and axle. It consists of the wheel (of course!) with an axle attached at its center. The axle is what keeps that wheel in place. When force is applied to either the wheel or the axle, they both rotate.

This invention is considered one of man's best. It has made work easier and play much more fun.

Wheels are obviously very helpful for moving things around. Without them, we'd have to push, pull, or carry EVERYTHING! We even move ourselves with wheels, on bicycles and cars, skateboards and buses.

ESSENTIAL QUESTION

How might history have been different without wheels?

ROLL BACK THE YEARS

Wheels are incredibly useful for transportation purposes, but historians think that the first wheels were used to make pottery, not for transportation. The pottery wheel was invented around 3500 BCE in Mesopotamia, an ancient civilization that was in an area that today is mostly in Iraq, and also in parts of Turkey, Iran, and Syria. The Mesopotamians found that wet clay could be formed into bowls and other containers if it sat upon a turning wheel while the potter's hands manipulated the material.

It wasn't until about 300 years later that someone got the idea to use the wheel to move things. Then, they were used for **chariots**. The Greeks later invented the wheelbarrow to help carry loads of materials or tools. **Watermills** and **windmills** were also invented using the wheel. Spinning wheels emerged to make yarn and string. And the rest is history.

Wheels are entirely **MANMADE**.
They do not exist in nature. The closest thing might be the **ROLY POLY BUG**, because it sometimes rolls to move, or the
DUNG BEETLE that rolls dung into a ball to move it.

credit: ocean yamaha
(CC BY 2.0)

You can probably list many examples of wheels and axles. Bikes, roller skates, skateboards, and scooters have wheels. Planes, trains, and automobiles all have wheels. What else?

Had any pizza lately? The slice was probably cut with a pizza cutter, which is another example of a wheel and axle. A rolling pin is another. Merry-go-rounds, revolving doors, and fans all use a wheel and axle, too. Do you have a hamster or gerbil? If so, you probably have an exercise wheel in there for the little critter.

What other examples of wheels and axles can you find in your home? In your neighborhood?

WHEELBARROWS are actually a clever combination of two simple machines: **WHEELS** and **LEVERS**. The long handles of the wheelbarrow (the levers) make it much **EASIER TO LIFT** the load and the wheels **REDUCE** the **FRICTION**, making it much **EASIER TO MOVE**.

Hot Wheels Cars

Not only are Hot Wheels cars loads of fun to play with, they are also a key ingredient when building contraptions. In 2018, the toy car brand celebrated its 50th birthday. Ruth (1938–2002) and Elliot Handler (1916–2011) cofounded the Mattel toy company. Ruth invented the Barbie doll in the late 1950s, inspiring Elliot to want to develop a toy for boys that was as popular as the one his wife had invented for girls. Back then, many people thought boys and girls wanted different kinds of toys. Thus, the cars. Together with a real car designer and a rocket scientist, Elliot created a line of toy cars that were better than other cars available at the time. The first "Sweet 16" cars were launched in 1968. Those 16 cars were modeled after some of the most notable real cars of the time. The very first was the Custom Camaro. Since then, the company has designed more than 25,000 models. And most likely, you or someone you know has one you can use in your contraptions.

HOW WHEELS AND AXLES HELP

Suppose you have to move a heavy box of books. The box is too heavy to even lift. When it is on the ground, you have to use a lot of force to push the box along. This is extremely hard because you have two forces working against you: friction and gravity.

Friction resists the movement of the box of books along the ground. And gravity pulls the box downward while you are trying to move it in a different direction—forward.

What happens when you put that box of books on a cart with wheels? The whole process becomes much easier! When you put a load on wheels, it reduces the amount of friction working against you. The cart you use to move the stack of books will reduce friction, which, in turn, lessens the amount of force you must apply to move the stack.

CRAZY CONTRAPTIONS

shaft: a long, narrow rod that forms the handle of a tool or club.

World's Fair: an international show to exhibit the achievements of countries from around the world and get a glimpse at the future.

Another reason using the cart makes the work easier is because wheels and axles provide a mechanical advantage. This is true of all simple machines. The wheel and axle make work easier by requiring you to use less force over a greater distance. That means the bigger the wheel, the more the force will be multiplied. So, when you go to get a cart to move those books, look for the one with the biggest wheels!

This video, published by Hot Wheels, features cars and tracks in a contraption designed to turn on a television. What simple machines can you spot in use?

🔎 Hot Wheels Goldberg

PS

Wheels and axles can work in two different ways. You can apply the force to the axle, which then turns the wheel. An example of this is the Ferris wheel. The force is applied to the axle in the center, which then turns the giant wheel, lifting kids up high in the air. Car wheels move this way, too. And, when you ride a bicycle, you are also applying force to the axle, which spins the wheels to send you on an adventure.

The other way to use wheels and axles is to apply the force to the wheel, which then turns the axle. Believe it or not, a screwdriver is an example of a wheel and axle used in this way. The handle is the wheel. The screwdriver's **shaft** is the axle.

Doorknobs also apply force to the wheel to turn the axle. The knob is the wheel that turns the axle inside the door. Ask an adult to help you take apart a doorknob in your home. Watch the wheel and axle at work!

Using wheels and axles in contraptions adds a whole new element to your designs. Start thinking about things you already have that could be used as wheels and axles in your contraptions. Toy cars and trains are an easy place to start. What else could you use? What can you make?

ESSENTIAL QUESTION

How might history have been different without wheels?

Ferris Wheels

Today, Ferris wheels are a common attraction at fairs, carnivals, and amusement parks. We have George Washington Gale Ferris Jr. (1859–1896) to thank for this! The inventor wanted to create an attraction for the 1893 **World's Fair** in Chicago that was as popular and awe-inspiring as the Eiffel Tower had been four years earlier in Paris, France. He sketched and sketched and sketched. He wanted to capture every detail in the design before it went into production.

Finally, the result of all his brainstorming was a rotating wheel on two, 140-foot-tall steel towers. It had a 45-foot-long axle through the wheel, between the towers. The wheel itself had a 250-foot diameter and 35 wooden cars. Each car held up to 60 people. The wheel could carry 2,160 people at a time! The structure was lit by another new invention—the light bulb—3,000 of them to be exact. Not only was this first Ferris wheel a big success at the fair, but it was also an engineering sensation.

The original Ferris wheel in 1893

WATER THE
PLANT

Before wheels were commonplace, some ancient civilizations used logs to move heavy objects in a similar way that wheels might have done. Here's how. Several logs were placed parallel to one another. Then, the load was placed on the logs. When a force was applied to the load, the logs rolled. As with a wheel and axle, the rolling logs reduced the friction. They also reduced the amount of force needed to move the object. Even today, you can see this concept in action in rollers that are part of a **conveyor belt** system.

Time to experiment with this primitive wheel and see how rolling logs can help move something.

The Challenge Identified: Start with the idea of using rolling logs to move something heavy. In this case, have your heavy object tilt a cup of water to water a plant.

> **ALERT:** This could get a little messy. Have some old towels on hand to clean up with or move the contraption outside!

❯ **Brainstorm ideas and supplies:** You probably don't have a stack of logs on hand. If so, go for it! Otherwise, find smaller things that can simulate rolling logs. Lincoln Logs? Pencils? TP rolls? You also need a heavy object. You could use a book or a brick or a block of wood.

❯ **Draw a plan:** This is a pretty simple challenge, but ideally it will show you how ancient people used logs to move things along. It will also give you another element to add to your larger, more complex contraptions later on.

WORDS TO KNOW

conveyor belt: a system that uses a moving band of fabric, rubber, or metal to move objects easily; often seen in factories or in airports.

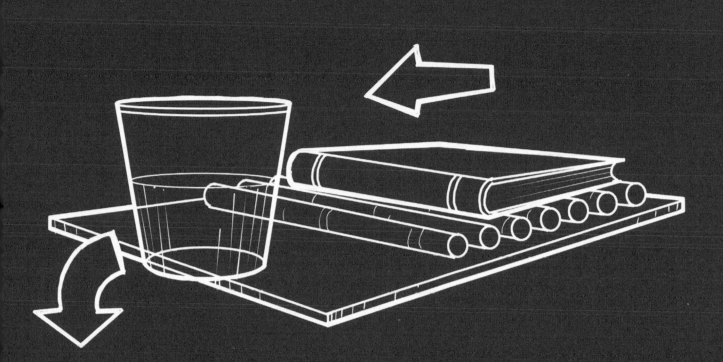

Build: Put this mini-contraption together by lining up your "logs," getting a cup of water, and setting a plant in just the right spot.

Test: Send that heavy object rolling across the logs!

Evaluate: Not as easy as it sounded, was it? Perhaps you didn't use enough force to move the heavy object toward the cup of water. Or maybe you used too much force. Did the cup tip over the way you wanted it to or did the cup itself land in the plant? And, did the water end up on the plant? Or everywhere else?

Redesign? If you try it again, you may want to create a frame around your "logs" to keep them moving in the right direction. You might try using different material for the logs. Tipping the cup a little when you set things up could help, too. And you may need to adjust the position of the plant so the water actually goes where you want it to!

CANDY
DELIVERY!

You may already have toys around that have wheels and axles. However, for this challenge, you will make your own.

The Challenge Identified: Make a balloon car to deliver candy to a friend across the table.

> **Brainstorm ideas and supplies:** You can make a car out of materials you find around your home. A simple one can be made from an empty toilet paper roll, two straws, four "wheels," some tape, glue, and a balloon. You will also need some candy to deliver. A candy bar could simply be taped to the top of the car. Or you could attach a cup or small box to the top of the car to deliver jelly beans or candy corn. Maybe you just want to put whatever you choose inside the car.

> **Draw a plan:** Focus on your car design first. Then, sketch out the whole contraption.

Contraption Hint: Many everyday objects make good wheels—you just have to keep your eyes open and be creative. And the more engineering and building you do, the more ideas will come to you. Here are a few suggestions: bolts, lids (from milk jugs, water bottles, yogurt containers), CDs (old ones!), buttons, and coins.

Build: Start by punching four holes in your TP roll where the axles will go through. Using a hole punch is an easy way to do this. There must be two holes in the front and two in the back. Next, cut one of the straws in two—each piece is an axle. The axles should stick out half an inch on each side of the TP roll. Use hot glue to attach the wheels to the axle. Try to center the axle on the wheel or your car will be wobbly.

Tape a straw lengthwise, front to back across the top of the car. The straw should stick out over both ends. On one end, attach an uninflated balloon to the straw. Make sure the seal is tight. If you are attaching candy or a box, attach those securely on the top.

❱ **Test:** Once your car is built and your candy is ready for delivery, blow up the balloon. You will want to pinch the straw closed when you are done so the air doesn't escape as you set the car down. Then, let go!

❱ **Evaluate:** What did you learn about building a car? Not as easy as it looks? Was your axle centered on your wheels? Were the holes in the TP roll in the right place for the axle to pass through? Did your wheels even stay on? Did the balloon create enough force as the air escaped? The seal around the balloon, where it attaches to the straw, may need to be tightened. Your car may or may not have gone in the direction you wanted. What could you do to make the car move in the direction you want it to?

❱ **Redesign?** If your car didn't move like you wanted it to, how could you redesign it? Look closely at your car as it goes to determine what isn't working. What can you do to make it more sturdy? Move more efficiently? Perhaps experiment with the size of the balloon you use and how much you inflate it.

Build Your Own Car

There are many, many ways to make your own car, balloon-powered or not. Browse the internet for ideas. **Here are a few good places to start.**

🔍 frugal fun car craft

🔍 video car clothespin

🔍 Scientific America balloon car

🔍 TP Roll Race Cars

SEND A
MESSAGE

You now know about three different simple machines. This time, you will use an inclined plane, a wheel and axle, and a lever to create a contraption.

The Challenge Identified: Create a contraption using at least one lever, one inclined plane, and one wheel to display a message.

▶ **Brainstorm ideas and supplies:** Get out the levers, inclined planes, and wheels and axles you've already used or find or make new ones. How can you combine these three simple machines in a contraption?

▶ **Draw a plan:** What will start your chain reaction? What will happen next? This contraption is an example of how it might look.

▶ **Build:** Put your three simple machines together and have your message ready for display.

▶ **Test:** Start the chain reaction.

Contraption Hint: Sometimes, engineers and other creators find it necessary to use **backward design**. That means starting with what you want to accomplish. In this case, first decide what message you want to display and how you might go about displaying it. Next, plan the step before that. Then keep thinking backward from there.

WORDS TO KNOW

backward design: the process of creating something starting with identifying what you want to accomplish, in order to determine the process needed to reach that goal.

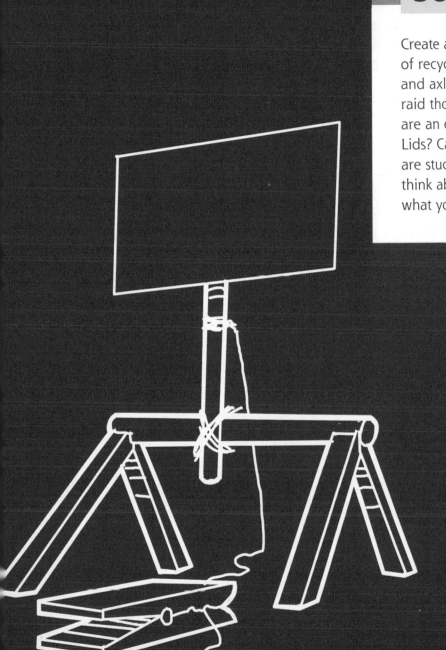

Create a five-step contraption ENTIRELY out of recycled materials, including the wheels and axles. You can add glue and tape. Go raid the recycling! Paper towel and TP rolls are an excellent start. What else is in there? Lids? Cans? Cardboard? No cheating! If you are stuck because you don't have something, think about how you could make it out of what you do have.

Evaluate: Did it operate like you expected? Did one part perform better than another part? Were the forces enough to keep things moving? Did your message display like you wanted it to?

Redesign? Does your contraption need an overhaul? Maybe it just needs a few minor adjustments. You might even want to redesign it and add more elements. Or you might want to think of other ways to display a message, or even more than one message.

Chapter 5

PLUCKY

PULLEYS

Some simple machines are made up of other simple machines! For example, the pulley. Do you have the kind of window blinds that can be raised and lowered with a rope? Have you ever gotten to raise the flag on the pole outside your school? Have you ever been ziplining? If so, you probably used a pulley.

The pulley consists of a wheel (sometimes with a groove on the rim) combined with a rope, chain, belt, or cord. It helps to raise, lower, and move objects.

Some of the first people to use a pulley were the same Mesopotamians who first used the wheel and axle. It's believed that these ancient people used a pulley to lift water as early as 1500 BCE. Historians think that even before this, people used ropes or vines swung over tree limbs as **makeshift** pulleys.

ESSENTIAL QUESTION

What are some inventions made possible by pulleys?

Yet the person who gets the most credit for the invention of the pulley is Archimedes—remember, he also demonstrated how levers help do work. Plus, you'll see him again in the chapter about screws. Archimedes was the ancient Greek mathematician and inventor. He was the one who actually explained the mechanical advantage of pulleys and spent considerable time demonstrating his **theories**.

WORDS TO KNOW

makeshift: using whatever is around as a temporary substitute.

theory: an unproven idea that explains why something is the way it is.

GOING UP?

ARCHIMEDES used a rope and pulley system that was **POWERED BY** men or animals.

If you look at the history of humankind, you'll see that simple machines have played enormous roles in defining the world we live in today. The pulley is no exception. For an example, let's take a look at elevators.

Elevators might seem like a modern invention. However, the very first basic elevators were used thousands of years ago. Archimedes (him again!) built a simple elevator to lift heavy goods and materials during the third century BCE. The first known elevator for human use was installed for King Louis XV in 1743. This elevator in the Palace of Versailles in France was known as "the flying chair." To use it, the king pulled a cord attached to counterweights that were connected to a pulley system.

WORDS TO KNOW

steam engine: an engine powered by steam created by heating water.

Industrial Revolution: a period of time beginning in the late 1700s when people started using machines to make things in large factories.

gladiator: a warrior in ancient Rome who fought other gladiators or animals as a form of public entertainment.

fixed pulley: a pulley system in which the pulley is fixed to a point and the rope is attached to the load or object.

moveable pulley: a pulley system in which the load is attached directly to the pulley. One end of the rope is fixed to a point, and the other end of the rope can be free or fixed.

Outdoor Elevator

The Zhangjiajie National Forest Park, in the Hunan Province of China, is comprised of many remarkable sandstone pillars. These pillars rise above the forest floor as much as 3,000 feet. To offer visitors a full view of the pillars and surrounding forest at the national park, there is an elevator. This outdoor elevator is built into the cliff and stretches 1,070 feet (326 meters). There are three parallel cars running up and down the cliff face. Each one can carry 50 passengers. It can travel to the top (or bottom) in one minute and 32 seconds.

A big step in elevator technology occurred after the invention of the **steam engine** in 1765. With the help of the steam engine, elevators could lift bigger, heavier loads to the increasingly taller buildings that were being erected during the **Industrial Revolution**. At that time, though, most elevators were not for human use. This was because the rope or cable attached to the elevator could fray and snap, causing death and disaster. Finally, in 1852, the safety brake was introduced. By 1857, the very first passenger elevator was installed in a department store in New York City.

In **ANCIENT ROME**, simple lifts were used in the Roman Coliseum to raise the **WILD ANIMALS** from the lower level to the arena level, where they faced off against **gladiators**.

The Palace of Versailles was certainly large enough to warrant an elevator!

The first electric elevators appeared in the 1880s. Since then, elevators have continued to move more and more people to greater and greater heights at faster and faster speeds. And all because of the pulley.

PULLEY CONSTRUCTION

Most pulleys have a wheel with a groove around the rim. A rope, chain, belt, or cord sits in that groove, which keeps it in place. The wheels of pulleys can be any size, from very tiny to the gigantic pulley wheels used in construction. The length of the rope, chain, belt, or cord can also be any size or length, depending on the job.

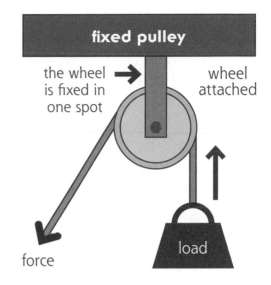

fixed pulley

the wheel is fixed in one spot

wheel attached

load

force

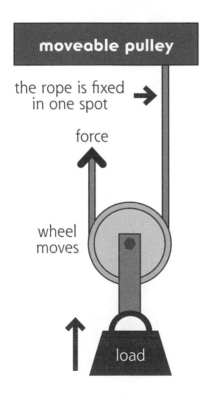

moveable pulley

the rope is fixed in one spot

force

wheel moves

load

There are different kinds of pulleys. The simplest is the **fixed pulley**. Just as the name suggests, this type of pulley is attached in one place.

As mentioned, raising the flag uses a fixed pulley. If you have curtains in your home, opening and closing them uses a fixed pulley system, too. Sailors sometimes use fixed pulleys to raise and lower sails. You will use this type of pulley to raise and lower elements of your contraptions.

There are also **moveable pulleys**. You guessed it, this kind of pulley moves. In this case, the pulley sits on the rope and the load is attached to the pulley. At least one end of the rope is attached to a fixed point and the pulley moves on the rope.

WORDS TO KNOW

compound pulley: a pulley system that includes both a fixed and a moveable pulley.

Some elevators and cranes use a moveable pulley. Ziplines are a type of moveable pulley, too. The pulley runs along the cable moving the load, which is YOU!

If you combine a fixed pulley and a moveable pulley, you have a **compound pulley**. This type of pulley can frequently be found on construction sites, where cranes are used to lift heavy materials. Modern elevators use this type of pulley, too. Weightlifting equipment sometimes uses compound pulley systems as well.

Look around you. In addition to the pulleys used for flags and curtains, they are also used on cranes. Ski lifts run on pulleys and large cables. What else? Can you find any other examples of pulleys at home? In your school? Your community?

ARCHIMEDES was one of the first people to use a compound pulley. He moved an **ENTIRE WARSHIP** full of men to demonstrate how the compound pulley can help us do work.

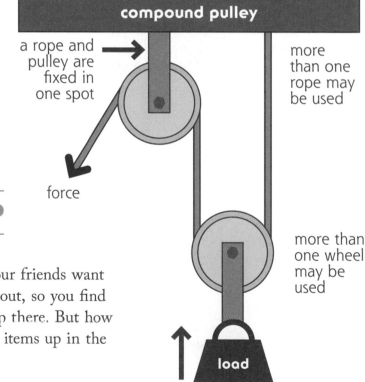

compound pulley

a rope and pulley are fixed in one spot

force

more than one rope may be used

more than one wheel may be used

load

HOW PULLEYS HELP

Imagine a treehouse. You and your friends want to make it a great place to hang out, so you find a small table and chairs to put up there. But how are you going to get those heavy items up in the trees? With a pulley!

Even if you don't have a proper pulley, simply slinging a rope over a high branch will work like a fixed pulley. The branch must be higher than your treehouse platform to work. Once the rope is in place, you can tie a chair to one end of the rope. You pull on the other end.

Fixed pulleys such as this don't change the amount of force you need to raise the load (the chair). However, they change the direction of the applied force. In this case, you pull down on the rope to raise the chair up, in the same way you would raise a flag on a flagpole. Even though there is no mechanical advantage to using this kind of pulley in terms of the force needed to lift the chair, it is still easier than trying to lift the chair by hand.

To get a better understanding of how pulleys work, watch this PBS video.

PBS kids pulley work

PS

Not only that, you can lift the chair to heights much taller than yourself. You can also use your weight to apply force—if you weigh more than the chair. The force of gravity helps you pull down on the rope, too. If you are lucky enough to have a proper pulley that includes a wheel with a grooved rim, the wheel will reduce the friction on the rope.

Moveable pulleys are even better because they do have a mechanical advantage. They reduce by half the amount of force you need to raise, lower, or move something. That means that you can lift something even heavier than the chair—even something heavier than yourself.

WORDS TO KNOW

bloomers: old-fashioned loose pants for women and girls that are gathered at the knee or ankle.

pegboard: a board with an evenly spaced pattern of small holes for pegs.

mining: taking minerals, such as coal or gold, from the ground.

You can even find **PULLEYS** in **SLIDING DOORS!** Do you have any doors in your house that slide instead of swing open? These are hanging on pulleys that let the door ease open and closed along its tracks.

In a moveable pulley type of system, one end of the rope is attached to a set point. The pulley on the rope is attached to whatever load you want to move. In some cases, the other end is free (or in your hand!). Because more sections of the rope are supporting the load, it is like having a friend help you carry a heavy box. The only problem is that to lift something with a single moveable pulley, you have to lift up on the rope, which is more difficult than pulling down on it.

Pulleys in Clothing

Following the invention of the bicycle in the early 1800s, this new form of transportation grew in popularity. For women, it was a source of freedom. But there was one problem—clothing. Women at the time wore long, layered skirts. That made cycling tricky, not to mention a bit dangerous if the material were to get caught in the wheels or pedals. There were even numerous accounts in newspapers of women being injured or even killed in bike crashes caused by clothing. Yet women were not to be deterred. Some simply wore **bloomers**, despite the fact that was not considered "proper" attire for women. Others came up with new forms of bicycle clothing to solve the dress problem.

One such idea involved pulleys! In 1895, Alice Bygrave filed a patent for her "Improvements in Ladies' Cycling Skirts" in the United Kingdom. Alice was a dressmaker. She invented a skirt that had a double pulley system. The pulleys were sewn into the front and back seams of a skirt. That way, the wearer could adjust the height of the hemline. Before getting on the bicycle, the rider raised the skirt to keep it out of the way. When she stepped off the bike, she could lower it to the proper, socially acceptable length. Innovative!

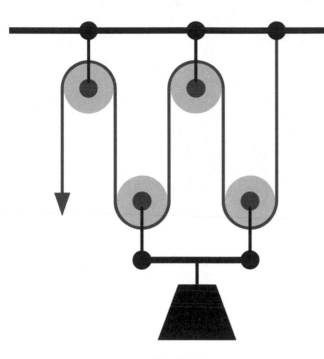

Compound Pulley in Action

Watch the adventures of a green ball as it moves up and down on the **pegboard**-mounted contraption. How many pulleys can you count?

🔎 Sprice machine green

PS

Some of the **WORLD'S LARGEST PULLEY** systems are used in **mining**. They help bring heavy loads to the surface smoothly and efficiently.

Other times though, both ends of the rope are fixed to a point. Then, the pulley loaded with the object rides along the rope when a force is applied. This is how ziplines work.

Now, if you were to rig a compound pulley system, you could not only change the direction of the force you apply but you could also continue to reduce the amount of force needed. Compound pulleys provide the greatest mechanical advantage. Each time you add a pulley to the system, you increase the amount of rope needed. This decreases the amount of force needed to move an object. Therefore, you will be able to lift heavier and heavier objects. The reason for this is that you are spreading the work out over a distance (sound familiar?), on a longer and longer rope.

Pulleys are a great addition to any contraption. Not only can they help raise or lower things, they can also move things around. In this way, they can help the motion in your chain reaction go sideways, up, and down.

ESSENTIAL QUESTION

What are some inventions made possible by pulleys?

RAISE THE
FLAG

Since the pulley system on a flagpole is one we see in everyday life, let's start there. This challenge will use only one, fixed pulley. But don't worry, the challenges will get more complicated!

The Challenged Identified: Create a contraption of at least three steps that raises a miniature flag on a miniature flagpole using either real or makeshift pulleys.

▶ **Brainstorm ideas and supplies:** You'll need something for a base, something for the pole, rope or string, and something to act as a pulley. Then, decide what chain reaction you will use to raise your flag. And don't forget the flag, which can be made out of fabric or paper or many other materials!

Contraption Hint: You don't need actual pulleys to make a contraption using pulleys. Many objects can serve as a grooved wheel that a string can pass over to create a fixed pulley. Empty thread or wire spools, push pins, and small Lincoln Logs can all act as pulleys. Or look through a collection of art supplies, a Lego bin, or train set for something to use. Also, don't forget that ancient peoples most likely used a makeshift pulley by throwing a rope or vine over a branch. How can you copy that in your contraption?

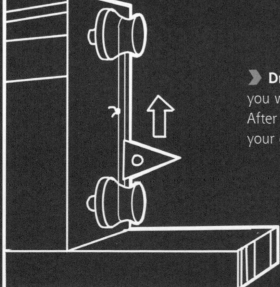

▶ **Draw a plan:** Start by sketching out how you will make a flagpole and pulley system. After that, add the rest of the contraption to your drawing.

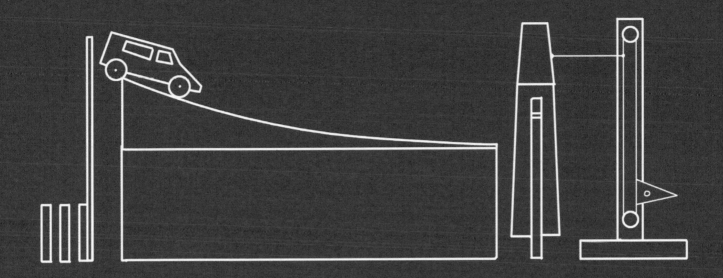

Build: Put the contraption together so your flag can be raised using the pulley system that you've designed.

Test: Once you've built your flagpole, attached a flag, and set up the chain reaction that will raise it (maybe), try it out. Your chain reaction might include a row of falling dominoes that finally lands on a pencil that's holding up a block of wood, onto which the rope end is stuck. When the block of wood falls, the flag goes up thanks to the pulley.

Evaluate: Did the flag rise like you wanted it to? Why or why not? Was the flagpole sturdy enough? Maybe there wasn't enough force to raise the flag. Or maybe there was too much!

Redesign? What design changes can you make to your pulley system to make it more effective? Do you need to make your flagpole stronger? Or perhaps think of other materials you could use to make a flagpole or contraption to start the flag raising. Lessening the tension on the string might also make the flag easier to raise.

ZIPPERING
ZIP LINES

Remember, ziplines are a type of moveable pulley. And they sure are fun to ride! Not only that, they make a great addition to crazy contraptions. Once you learn how to incorporate them into your designs, you won't want to stop.

The Challenge Identified: Make a zipline to use in a contraption of more than five steps that will zip a zipper.

▶ **Brainstorm ideas and supplies:** You need a zipline "cable." What will you use? It doesn't have to be long, but it needs to be strung between two points, probably with one end higher than the other. What will you attach your cable to? You also need a pulley. If you don't have one, you can make a simple one. It just has to move down your cable. Maybe you have some toys that have pulleys. You also need to find something with a zipper.

▶ **Draw a plan:** Commit your idea to paper. Here's one possibility.

▶ **Build it:** String up that cable, make a pulley or attach one, and get ready to zip.

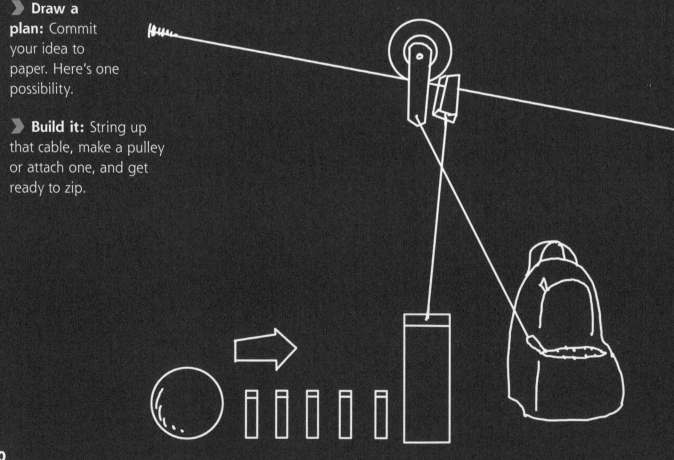

Build Your Own Pulley

Pulleys and ziplines are easy to make using materials you already have at home. There are many examples online. **Try these or search for "DIY pulley craft."**

🔍 Goldfish crackers STEAM

🔍 Sciencing crane

🔍 LEGO zipline

🔍 zipline toy mini

❯ **Test:** Bring your pulley to the top of the zipline. Then, let go!

❯ **Evaluate:** How did your pulley perform? If you used a real pulley and it didn't stay on the cable, maybe you need more weight hanging from it. If you made a pulley, did it move along like you wanted? Maybe there was too much friction or not enough weight. Maybe the start point on the zipline wasn't high enough. Finally, was there enough force to zip the zipper?

❯ **Redesign?** If things didn't go quite like you wanted, go back to the drawing board. How could you improve your pulley? What could you do to the zipline to make it more effective? Also consider using the zipline in a different place in the contraption; if it was at the end, move it to the middle. If it was at the beginning, maybe move it to the end.

ROLL THE
DICE

Things are getting interesting! Now that you know about pulleys and how they operate, you can combine them with the other simple machines you've used.

The Challenge Identified: Make a contraption with a minimum of five steps, using at least one inclined plane, one lever, one wheel and axle, and one pulley to roll a set of dice.

❯ **Brainstorm ideas and supplies:** Start with the dice—that's easy. If you don't have any, you can make them out of paper (search online for a template with the keywords "make dice"). Think about the other simple machines you've made and used. How can you put them together? How will you get the dice to roll?

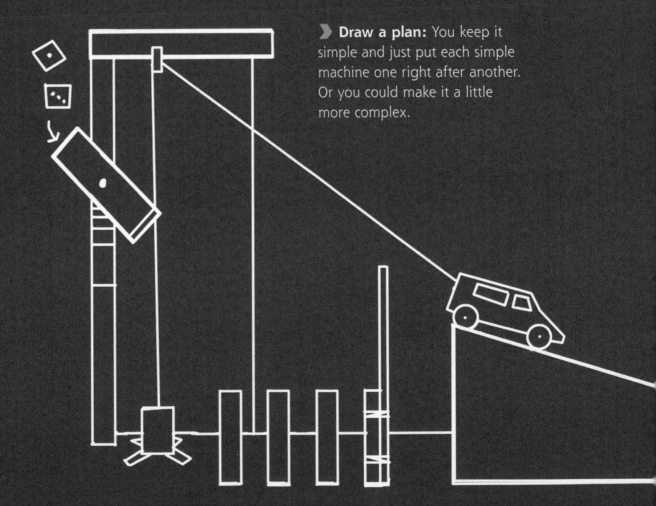

❯ **Draw a plan:** You keep it simple and just put each simple machine one right after another. Or you could make it a little more complex.

Build: Put the elements together. Get the dice ready. Get ready to rock and roll!

Test: Set the simple machines in motion.

Evaluate: Did the dice roll like you expected? How well did the different simple machines work together? Were there parts that performed well and others that didn't? Were the forces transferred throughout your contraption?

Redesign? If your contraption worked well, maybe you want to add more elements or have some of the elements repeat. Maybe some of the simple machines didn't work together. What improvements could you make? As you built the contraption or watched it in motion, did you get any new ideas about how to put elements together?

SUPER CHALLENGE

Make a compound pulley that lifts something heavy. If you have actual pulleys, great. If not, make some. Experiment. Don't forget to consider that whatever you build your pulleys on will need to be strong enough to support the weight of whatever you are going to lift.

Chapter 6

WILD ABOUT
WEDGES

Have you used your teeth to bite into an apple lately? A burger? A piece of pie? Your front teeth act as a wedge! You probably won't be using your teeth to build contraptions, but wedges are extremely helpful when engineering crazy contraptions. In real life, wedges can split something apart (like that burger), separate two things, or hold objects in place.

Wedges come in many forms and in all sizes. Most wedges look like two inclined planes back to back—wide at one end and coming to a sharp point at the other. Some of the oldest forms of wedges (besides teeth!) were used during the Stone Age—that was more than 2 million years ago! Early people used cutting tools that were wedges made of stone.

ESSENTIAL QUESTION

How do wedges help people do work?

The word **WEDGE** can also refer to a type of **GOLF CLUB**, a hairstyle, a shoe, or a **SLICE OF PIE**! It can be used as a **VERB**, too.

These simple machines probably helped them cut meat to eat or cut wood for fires. Have you ever seen or found a Native American **arrowhead**? That is another example of a wedge used by early civilizations. Arrowheads were fastened to the end of spears or arrows and used for hunting.

In fact, any tool used for cutting is considered a wedge. A **chisel** is another form of wedge. Its usefulness can be seen in marble statues created throughout history.

Today, wedges are still a big part of our everyday lives. We use axes to split wood. And knives help us cut our food. Ice picks help us break up ice. The bow of a ship is shaped like a wedge, letting a ship cut through the surface of the water more easily. Same thing with the nose of an airplane. It helps the plane cut through the air just as a knife helps to cut food.

WEIRD WEDGES

Sure, axes, teeth, and knives all have a wedge shape, no matter how small. But there are other wedges that you might not think to categorize as such. What about nails and thumbtacks? Wedges!

WORDS TO KNOW

superfluous: more than is necessary or wanted.

precise: exact, very accurate.

snips: a type of hand-held shears used for cutting sheet metal.

shears: a type of scissors with longer blades that are generally used for cutting heavy material.

These wedges help us hold objects in place. A door stop is another example of this type of wedge. What other examples of wedges can you find around you?

How about scissors? The first types of scissors appeared in the Middle East more than 3,000 years ago! These "spring scissors" worked much like tweezers do today. The two bronze blades were connected by a thin strip of bronze. When squeezed, the two blades came together to cut something. When released, the blades separated. Scissors were later adapted and used in ancient Rome, China, Japan, and Korea.

Michelangelo's *David*

One of the most famous statues carved from marble is called *David*. It was created by the famous Italian artist, Michelangelo (1475–1564). When he started the project in 1501, he simply had an enormous block of marble. In his mind, though, Michelangelo knew what was in the stone. He said, "The sculpture is already complete within the marble block, before I start my work. It is already there, I just have to chisel away the **superfluous** material." Michelangelo would not have been able to create *David* without a chisel and other types of wedges. He used specific tools to break away the first large pieces of marble. Then, he used different tools to make more **precise** cuts. Michelangelo also understood how to apply the right amount of force in just the right place to reveal the sculpture. *David* was finished in 1504 and is considered one of the world's greatest masterpieces. It is admired not only for its size and portrayal of the human figure, but also for the intricate details.

The history of scissors is pretty amazing! There are even museums dedicated to these very important tools. **Take a look at this online article to see pictures of different types of scissors.** How have they evolved as centuries passed? What kinds of different jobs have scissors been used to do in different cultures?

🔎 Gizmodo scissors evolution

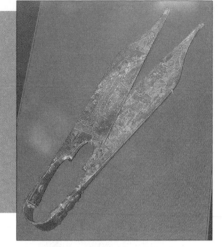

Spring scissors from Turkey, circa second century
credit: Yannick Trottier (CC BY 2.5)

The scissors we are familiar with today are called "pivoted scissors." The blades are connected at a point between the handles and the tips, and they pivot when the scissors are opened and closed. These scissors come in all shapes and sizes.

Scissors are commonplace in homes, schools, and businesses, most often to cut paper. People also use them in the kitchen to cut vegetables, meats, and other foods. Doctors use them, too. There are also scissors for cutting fabric, **snips** for cutting sheet metals, and pruning **shears** used in yards and gardens. Scissors are useful for all kinds of jobs!

One more thing to think about is that while the blades of the scissors alone are a type of wedge, the scissors themselves are actually two first-class levers! The pivot point where they are attached is the fulcrum.

One company in China has been making scissors since the 1600s. Its founder, Zhang Jiasi, wanted to make scissors that combined **GOOD STEEL** and **EXCELLENT WORKMANSHIP**. To this day, the company strives to make scissors that are both **DURABLE** and **BEAUTIFUL**.

WORDS TO KNOW

output force: the amount of force exerted on an object by a simple machine.

HOW WEDGES HELP

You may be wondering how wedges help do work. Imagine collecting wood for a campfire. You may get lucky and find some downed tree limbs in the forest. But you also need some larger pieces if you want your fire to last. Can you move big tree trunks? No! The tree needs to be chopped into smaller, more manageable pieces. You can't do that with just your hands, that's for sure. This is where an axe is useful. As with all simple machines, using a wedge—the axe—will make the job easier. And you'll get to enjoy the campfire much sooner!

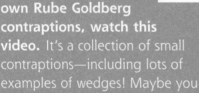

While you are learning about putting together your own Rube Goldberg contraptions, watch this video. It's a collection of small contraptions—including lots of examples of wedges! Maybe you'll be inspired to incorporate some of these mini-contraptions into your larger ones.

🔎 BigGame Tommy Goldberg

Wedges work by changing the direction of the force you apply. In fact, the force is applied in one direction and the result is an **output force** in two different directions.

When an adult goes to chop wood for your fire, they drive the axe down into the wood. The wedge redirects that force two ways and causes the wood to split. The axe turns the pushing force into a splitting force.

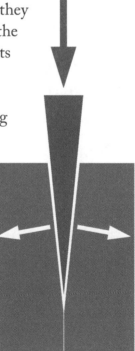

Not only that, when you apply force to the larger, wider end of the wedge, the wedge multiplies that force, while the narrow, sharp end of the wedge does the work. Your input force is applied over a long distance, which results in a greater output force over a short distance. This is the mechanical advantage of a wedge.

How much of a mechanical advantage you get when you use a wedge depends on how thick it is. If you have a short, thick wedge, you will be able to split things apart faster. However, you will need to use a lot of force. On the other hand, if you have a longer, thinner wedge, you will need to use less force to drive it in. This, though, takes more time.

Let's take a look at how nails work, too. At first glance, they don't really look like wedges. But look closer at the wide nail head. That is where you apply the force, usually with a hammer. The other end is a narrower, sharp point. The force is multiplied here, allowing the nail to move into the wood. Most of the time, you wouldn't be able to push a nail into a piece of wood by hand. The hammer, a type of lever, helps you to increase the force you apply, and the nail, the wedge, multiplies that force.

NAILS have been used by humans for more than 5,000 years. Early nails were made out of copper, bronze, and iron. Nails were made by hand until the eighteenth century. Even **THOMAS JEFFERSON MADE HIS OWN NAILS**. Today, nails are usually **FACTORY-MADE** out of steel and sometimes aluminum, iron, copper, or stainless steel.

Wedges are another essential element to add to contraptions. To start, wedges are good for holding parts in place until something happens to remove the wedges and free the parts so they can play their role in the contraption. You might use a wedge in front of a car at the top of an inclined plane or underneath a marble.

You might also use a wedge to separate two things. If a wedge is used in this manner, you can get the energy going in two different directions.

ESSENTIAL QUESTION

How do wedges help people do work?

TURN
THE PAGE

You may have already used a wedge in some of your earlier contraptions—if so, you probably already understand how valuable they can be! For this challenge, though, you are going to focus almost entirely on the wedge.

The Challenge Identified: Build a contraption using four wedges that hold objects in place. Design the contraption to turn the page of a book.

❯ **Brainstorm ideas and supplies:** Start by finding a book. That's easy. The harder part is thinking about how you will get the page of the book to turn—without harming the book!

❯ **Now, decide what you will use as wedges.** Will you make them out of a cereal box? Do you have triangle-shaped objects you can use? Do you have doorstops? In your contraption, you'll need to consider what object you want the wedges to hold in place. Perhaps you want to keep cars from going down a track. Or maybe you want to hold a marble in place. What else?

Contraption Hint: Don't have any wedges lying around? Well, make them. You can use cardboard (a cereal box is easy to cut and fold) to make a triangle-shaped wedge. It might look something like this.

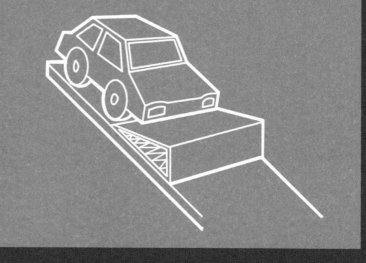

❯ **Draw a plan:** It could be something as simple as this idea with three wedges and five steps. Or you may want to get more complicated.

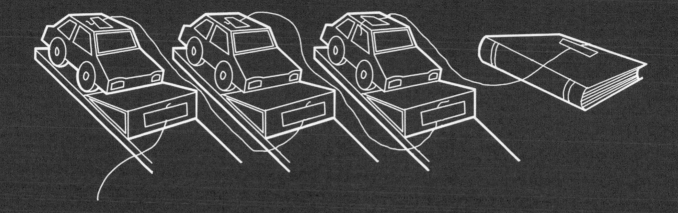

▶ **Build:** Set up your page-turning contraption. Put those wedges in place.

▶ **Test:** Put things in motion. Watch those wedges get pulled out of place and the page of your book turn.

▶ **Evaluate:** Start by evaluating the wedges. Did they work like you wanted? Was it trickier than expected to get the wedges to hold the objects in place? Was it tricky removing the wedges so the object could move? And did your page turn? Perhaps you needed more force to either remove the wedges or turn the page. How could you go about applying that force?

▶ **Redesign?** If you redesign this contraption, you may want to use different materials for the wedges. Or, if all four of your wedges were the same, maybe you want to make a contraption that uses four different wedges to hold things in place. Also, whether or not the wedges held objects in place and could be removed is due to the size of the wedge, so you may want to redesign them.

BOAT
LAUNCH

You've built a contraption using wedges to hold something in place. But don't forget, wedges can be used to split something or separate two things. Your next contraption should use this kind of wedge.

The Challenge Identified: Use a wedge to separate or split two things apart in a contraption with five or more steps that will launch a boat.

▶ **Brainstorm ideas and supplies:** You have wedges from the first challenge that you could use to hold an object in place. What will you use to split or separate things? No, don't use an axe. Even using a knife probably isn't a good idea. Unless . . . do you have a plastic knife? Or a block shaped like the head of an axe? You can also make one. Most importantly, you will need a boat and a tray of water.

Contraption Hint: No boat? No problem. You can make one. Popsicle sticks are great boat-building materials. Corks, too. Look around for items that could be used to make a small boat (think about stuff that floats). All you have to do for a cork boat is use two rubber bands to hold three corks together. Then, use a toothpick for a mast and a piece of paper for the sail. Done.

> **Draw a plan:** One idea may look like this. How else could you put the contraption together?

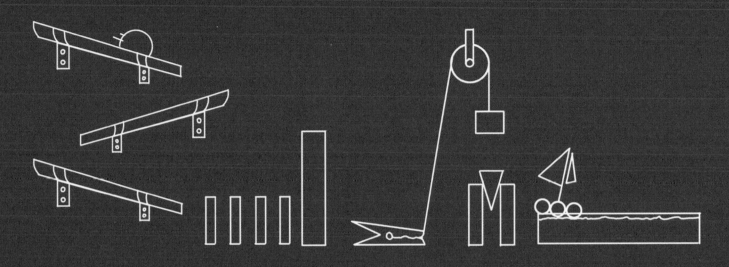

> **Build:** Fill your tray with water and moor your boat on the edge. Put all the other elements in place, including that wedge!

> **Test:** Your boat is ready to sail. Get it going.

> **Evaluate:** Did your boat launch? Did the wedge separate or split the items you used like you wanted it to? Did some parts of the contraption do what they were supposed to but not others? Was there enough force to move the boat across the water? Or maybe you now have water all over the place . . . too much force!

> **Redesign?** Is there a way to improve how the parts of the contraption work together? Or you might want to make the contraption more complicated or use a bigger tray of water and a bigger boat. Redesign it to make the contraption bigger and better!

TEA TIME!

Think back on the other simple machines you've learned about and used in contraptions. Ready to put them all together?

The Challenge Identified: Use an inclined plane, a wheel and axle, a lever, a pulley, and a wedge to build a contraption that will make tea—well, one that will at least dunk the teabag in the water.

❱ **Brainstorm ideas and supplies:** Start with the mug and the teabag. Then, decide what you will use for the other simple machines in this contraption. Do you still have some of the simple machines you used in earlier contraptions? Gather them up.

❱ **Draw a plan:** The planning stage is even more important as the contraptions get more challenging. Obviously, the last step is to dunk a teabag. But what will happen before that? Here's an idea!

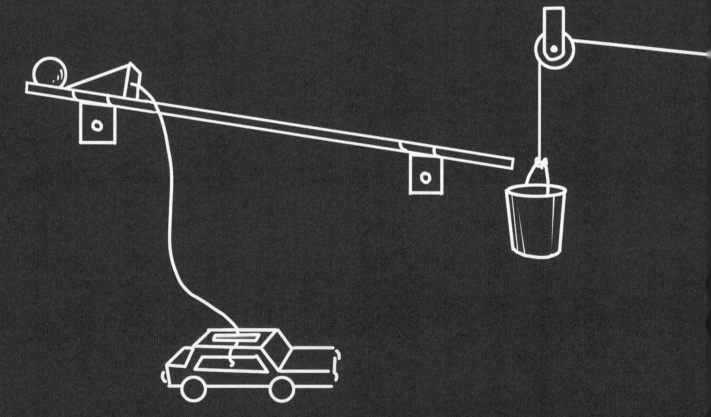

> **Build:** Assemble your contraption.

> **Test:** Tea time!

> **Evaluate:** Did all the simple machines work like they were supposed to? Did they work well together? Maybe some parts performed better than others. Did your teabag fall into the mug?

> **Redesign?** Perhaps you might reconfigure your contraption, putting the different simple machines in a different order. Or maybe it was close to dunking the teabag and just needs a little attention. You might even want to add one more of each simple machine to make it crazier.

SUPER CHALLENGE

Make your contraption **nonlinear**. In other words, make the forces of the chain reaction change direction at least five times. Or go for 10! In addition to changing direction on a single, flat surface, see if you can figure out how to make the motion in your contraption go down AND up.

For inspiration, check out one of Joseph's Machines—La Macchina Botanica—How to Water a Plant.

🔍 Macchina water plant

WORDS TO KNOW

nonlinear: not in a straight line.

Chapter 7

SAVVY ABOUT
SCREWS

Last but not least, the sixth simple machine—the screw. This is an ingenious machine, yet it's very simple. It's also been incredibly important to human history.

Examine a screw up close. What do you notice? A screw is really an inclined plane that wraps around a central axis, similar to a **helix**. The inclined plane winding around the axis creates the threads. Screws hold things together or help to lift a load.

Circular staircases are life-sized versions of a screw used to lift or lower a load. If you are on that staircase going up or down, that load is you! The circular staircase is a long, inclined plane that goes around and up—or down! Just as with an inclined plane, the circular staircase allows you to walk to another floor over a distance, which is easier than going straight up.

ESSENTIAL QUESTION

How have screws been used throughout history to make work easier?

That Greek mathematician Archimedes, who lived in the third century BCE, often gets the recognition for inventing the screw. Yes, he got the credit for the pulley, too, even though ancient peoples beat him to it. The same is true with the screw.

Evidence suggests that the first use of a screw actually happened in the seventh century BCE, several hundred years before Archimedes came along. Ancient texts and legends describe a screw-like irrigation system used to raise water to the Hanging Gardens of Babylon, found in Mesopotamia.

Archimedes, though, is the one who brought this system into more common use. And, since he is credited as the inventor, this primitive water pump is called the **Archimedes' screw**. This machine can lift water much more easily than a person lifting it by hand. It consists of a screw spiral inside a tube that sits at an angle. One end of the tube is placed in the water. At the upper end of the tube is a hand crank. By turning the crank, the water is lifted uphill against the force of gravity. The Archimedes' screw has been used throughout history for irrigation, to pull water out of leaky ships, and to removed water from flooded areas.

WORDS TO KNOW

helix: a three-dimensional shape that winds evenly around a central axis.

Archimedes' screw: a machine used to raise water to a higher lever for irrigation. It consists of a screw inside a **cylinder**, and as the screw turns, it raises the water.

cylinder: a solid figure with straight, parallel sides shaped into a circle or an oval, as in a can of soup or a paper towel roll.

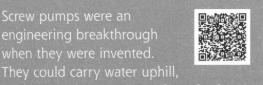

Screw pumps were an engineering breakthrough when they were invented. They could carry water uphill, working against gravity. **Take a look at this early version—a date tree!**

🔎 Archimedes' screw date tree

PS

WORDS TO KNOW

auger: a tool or device with a screw shaft that is used to make holes in wood, soil, ice, and other materials.

screw press: a device that uses the mechanical advantage of a screw to apply force.

terrace: a raised, flat platform or area of land.

native: belonging to an area or region.

archaeologist: a scientist who studies ancient people through the objects they left behind.

erosion: the gradual wearing away of rock or soil by water and wind.

After Archimedes, the screw was used more and more often and adapted to many different uses. In ancient Rome, for example, people used **augers** to bore holes in wood and other materials. This tool had a metal corkscrew attached to two wooden handles, forming a "T."

The screw was also used to press apples into cider or to make wine out of grapes. It was used to make olive oil, too. By using the screw to press fruit, more juice can be squeezed out than if doing it by hand.

When the printing press was invented in the fifteenth century, it used the same type of **screw press**. This invention sped up the printing process greatly.

Hanging Gardens of Babylon

The Hanging Gardens of Babylon are something of a legend. No one in the modern world has actually seen them. And there is no solid evidence that they truly existed. However, ancient writings describe lush, exotic gardens in the area that is now Iraq. As the story goes, they were built on orders from King Nebuchadnezzar II for his wife in the seventh century BCE. The fabled gardens were built on many levels of stone **terraces**. The terraces were planted with plants and trees. The gardens may have been as much as 80 feet high and covered an area 400 feet wide by 400 feet long. To water the gardens, irrigation would have been needed. That's where the Archimedes' screw came in. This primitive system would have provided thousands of gallons of water to the plants, which were not **native** to the area.

The existence of the Hanging Gardens is still debated today. While several writers from ancient Greece and Rome wrote about the gardens, **archaeologists** have not found any solid evidence. This could be due to earthquakes, wars, or **erosion**. There is also debate about the Hanging Gardens of Babylon's location and whether they were created by a different monarch in a different time. The truth remains a mystery.

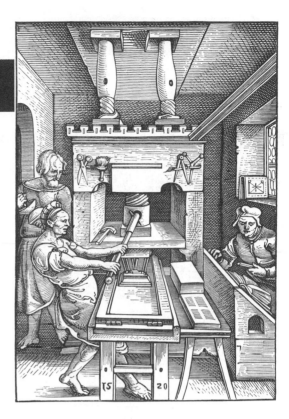

How many simple machines can you spot in this print from the sixteenth century?

Thanks to the printing press (and the screw!), books were manufactured faster and cheaper than ever before—so more people had access to them.

Around the same time, people began to make the metal screws, used as fasteners, that we are familiar with today. But at the time, these fasteners had to be made by hand. It wasn't until the 1800s that metal screws were made and used regularly, along with screwdrivers. Thanks to advances in technology, screws could be made by machines and always be the same.

Today, screws are very much a part of our everyday lives. They are used for many different purposes and come in a variety of sizes and shapes. The metal screw used to hold things together is the one we tend to think of first when we hear the word *screw*. But did you know that jars with twist-on lids are examples of a screw? Go find a jar. Take a look!

A wine press from the sixteenth century
credit: Chris Lake (CC BY 2.0)

ARCHIMEDES' SCREW was used in 2001 to help stabilize the **LEANING TOWER OF PISA**.

Both a jar and lid have threads. When the lid is screwed on, the jar and lid become interlocked. Look at a bottle cap, too, the next time you open a bottle. These are similar to jar lids, with screw threads on the lid and bottle.

As with screws, bolts have threads, too. Together with a nut, which also has screw threads, they hold things together. Light bulbs have screws on them as well—the screw tightens them in the socket. A drill bit is another example of a screw. Boat propellers and fans work like screws. And, of course, don't forget about the circular staircase. Now that you know what to look for, what else can you find?

HOW SCREWS HELP

Back to that circular staircase. It allows you to use less force to get upstairs than you would need to climb a pole or hoist yourself straight up. The amount of work is the same, but it is spread out over a distance, so you need less force. This is the same mechanical advantage you gain when you use an inclined plane.

The same thing happens when using a screw to hold things together. Not only do you input a small force across a longer distance, but the screw also changes the direction of the force.

The screw changes a turning force into a **linear** force. Plus, screws multiply the gentle input force of turning a screw into stronger downward output force.

Another benefit of a screw is that the threads of a screw grip the material around it, much like claws do. This creates a tight hold. The only way to get things apart is to unscrew the screw.

With screws, the mechanical advantage you gain depends on how far apart the threads are. Screws with threads close together will be easier to turn than a screw with threads further apart. However, when the threads are closer together, you have to turn the screw many more times to tighten it down. If the threads are further apart, you won't have to turn the screw as many times to tighten it. But you will need to apply more force.

The first use of a screw-on lid happened in 1858. A man named **JOHN LANDIS MASON** designed the lid to screw onto jars used for canning fruits and vegetables. The **MASON JAR** that bears his name is still around today!

Even General Mills, the company that makes cereal (among other things), was inspired by Rube Goldberg. In 2018, the company designed a series of boxes that could be turned into small Rube Goldberg machines!

🔎 General Mills Rube Goldberg

WORDS TO KNOW

funnel: a cone that opens to a tube at the narrow end to direct downward flow.

Once again, the choice is to work hard for a short amount of time or spend more time but not have to work as hard. There is an additional mechanical advantage when using a lever of some kind or screwdriver to turn the screw. As with all levers, the longer the lever, the more mechanical advantage.

Game On!

Rube Goldberg not only entertained millions of people with his contraption cartoons, he also inspired people. From movies to contests to artists, Rube Goldberg's legacy is evident. Even a board game was inspired by him. The game, *Mouse Trap*, was first produced by the Ideal Toy Co. in 1963. In the game, each player has a mouse that they move around the board. As players move their mice, they take turns building the Rube Goldberg-like mouse trap. Once assembled, the contraption includes inclined planes, a catapult, a wheel and axle with gears, and more. That's when players try to catch their opponents' mice. The last un-trapped mouse wins.

The game has been a family favorite for many years. It is still made today, manufactured by Hasbro. It's "the craziest trap you'll ever see." **You can view one of the old, original advertisements for the game at this website.**

🔎 Mouse Trap game first commercial

This is true not just for the traditional screws, but for all types of screws. If the "threads" (the stairs) on that circular staircase are close together, it will be easy to walk up. However, you will have to go around and around and around many times! Same with the light bulb. If the screws are far apart, you won't have to twist the bulb too many times to get it to fit in the socket.

Screws are fun to use in contraptions! Have you made a marble run yet? If you have, you might have already made something that can work like a screw. **Funnels** work like screws, too, because whatever is put in a funnel spirals around and around before emptying out the narrow opening at the bottom.

Most screws are designed to fasten in a CLOCKWISE direction. To tighten a screw or jar lid, you turn it to the right. To loosen, you turn it to the left. An easy way to remember this is to think, **"RIGHTY TIGHTY, LEFTY LOOSEY."**

You can always make screws for your contraptions! See if you have any old tubing around. The insulation used on pipes can be used to make a screw. Super bendy straws might also make good screws. Even empty toilet paper rolls can be cut and taped together to make a screw.

By now, you are an expert at finding everyday items to use. Wander around your home and find materials to use for a screw in a contraption.

Now, you've studied all six simple machines. It's time to use them all in a contraption! In the next chapter, you will continue to use what you know about the six simple machines to make even more complex Rube Goldberg machines.

ESSENTIAL QUESTION

How have screws been used throughout history to make work easier?

TURN ON
THE MUSIC

This challenge will give you a chance to play with a simple screw that winds around and around and around. Once you've experimented with the screw, you'll be able to use it in later contraptions.

The Challenge Identified: Create a five-step contraption to turn on a CD player (or iPod or radio or whatever device you use to listen to music). Use a track, long tube, marble run, or other material to spiral around a central axis like the threads on a screw at least three times.

❯ **Brainstorm ideas and supplies:** For your "screw" you could use a marble run. Or, if you want to make this challenge more challenging, use some other item to create a "screw" for a marble, ball, or toy car to roll down and around. To turn on a CD player you will need, well, a CD player (or other music device). What other elements might you want to use in your contraption?

❯ **Draw a plan:** Now that you have some experience designing crazy contraptions, have some fun with this step.

Build: Get that music device ready. Put the player in just the right spot. Build or assemble your screw. Put the other elements in place. **NOTE: Be very careful that you don't apply too much force to your device.**

Test: Get those parts moving!

Evaluate: Is your music playing? Is it time for a dance party or time for tweaking your contraption? You needed enough force to turn on the music, but not so much that it damaged the device. Were you successful? Did the screw work the way you wanted it to?

Contraption Hint: If you don't have a marble run at home, making or finding a screw can be a challenge but fun. Talk to someone at your local hardware store about the types of flexible tubing they sell. Or you might visit a recycled building or art materials business. One of the trickiest aspects may be finding a marble or ball small enough to run through the tube. Try using the small steel balls made for slingshots or using ball bearings, which come in all sizes and are often sold individually at the hardware store.

Redesign? Maybe you want to see if you can have the screw twist around four times or maybe five. Or perhaps you might want to experiment with other materials to use as a screw. And, certainly if the music isn't playing, you need to redesign or tweak your contraption.

Make an Archimedes' Screw

If you want to make your own screw, it's not too hard. **Here are a few examples that use different materials.**

slidesere Archimedes

Archimedes screw

create your own Archimedes

TIGHTEN
A LID

For this challenge, you will use a more traditional screw, though not the handheld, faster type. Instead, you will use the screw on the lid of a jar.

The Challenge Identified: Create a five-step contraption that screws the lid on a jar.

❯ **Brainstorm ideas and supplies:** Start by finding a jar and lid you can use. Plastic is better than glass. Or maybe you want to use a bottle with a screw-on cap. Make sure whatever you choose doesn't need too much force to screw it on. Also think about how levers apply an additional mechanical advantage to screws. Then, select the other elements you want in your contraption. What will apply the force to screw on the lid?

❯ **Draw a plan:** You may end up with a plan like this that includes a pull-back car and a circular track. Then again, you may have something different in mind.

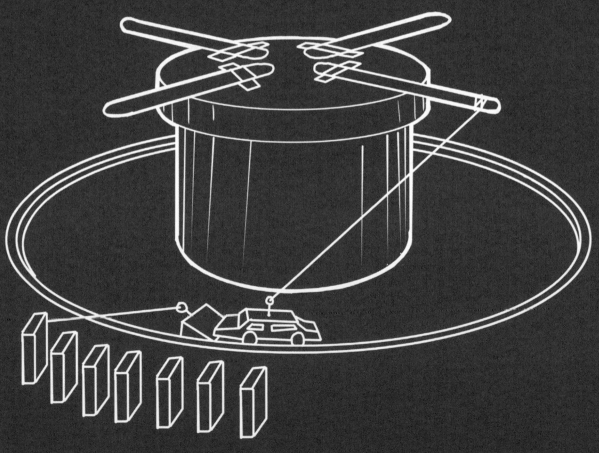

Build: Assemble your lid-screwing-on contraption.

Test: Start the chain reaction and tighten that lid.

Evaluate: Is the lid on tight? Maybe the lid was turned some, but not enough. You might need more force to get the lid to screw on tighter. Or maybe you need to rethink how you are applying the turning force.

Redesign? How else could you create a circular movement to screw the lid on a jar (without using hands!)? What other elements might you include? Can you make your contraption even more complicated?

A Contraption's Cousin

A close cousin to a Rube Goldberg contraption is a kinetic sculpture. This art form, which originated in the early twentieth century, incorporates movement into sculptures. Sometimes, the components are set in motion by a motor (not a chain reaction as in a contraption). But artists also use wind, water, smoke, steam, and **magnetism** to generate movement. If you look closely at these sculptures, you will see many of the same components as you use in making contraptions. Artists see these sculptures not just as objects but also as an event. Now that you've learned about forces and motion and simple machines, perhaps you might also try engineering a sculpture!

WORDS TO KNOW

magnetism: the force that attracts or repels between magnets.

POP!
GOES THE BALLOON

You probably guessed this was coming! It is now time to use all six simple machines in one contraption.

The Challenge Identified: Create a contraption of at least seven steps that includes an inclined plane, a wheel and axle, a lever, a pulley, a wedge, and a screw to pop a balloon.

❯ Brainstorm ideas and supplies: Start with the balloon and what you will use to pop it. Consider that whatever you use to pop the balloon may be a type of wedge. Then, look through all the contraption elements you've used throughout the book. Pull them out. How can each be used? Or maybe you want to use new ones.

❯ Draw a plan: This is one suggestion for how to put together a balloon-popping contraption.

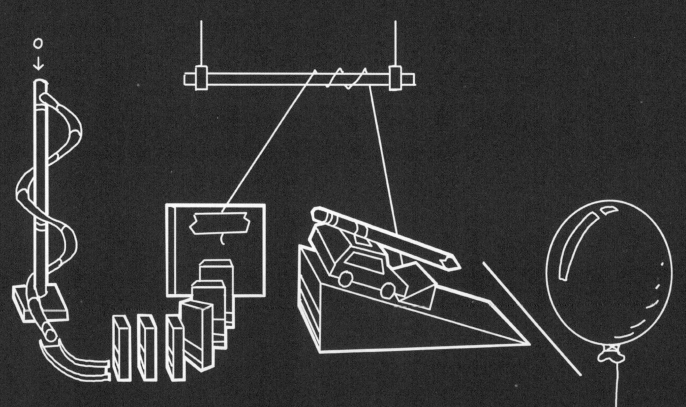

Balloon Fun

There is evidence that the first balloons were created by ancient peoples using animal intestines. The first rubber balloon was developed by a man named Michael Faraday in 1824. But he didn't invent it for fun. He created balloons to use for science experiments in his laboratory. By the middle part of the century, though, the idea of using balloons for fun and decoration caught on. People fill balloons with air, helium, or water, depending on the event. Nowadays, balloons come all shapes and sizes. Today, you can also find balloon artists who will twist and shape long, tubular balloons into different sculptures. And you can find contraption designers using balloons in their Rube Goldberg machines!

❯ **Build:** Blow up that balloon and put all those simple machines in place.

❯ **Test:** Ready, set, GO!

❯ **Evaluate:** Do you still have an inflated balloon? If so, perhaps there wasn't enough force to pop it. Or maybe whatever you used as the balloon popper wasn't sharp enough. You might need to inflate the balloon more to make it easier to pop. How did all your elements work together?

❯ **Redesign?** If things didn't go well, you will want to tweak your design to improve it. Or you may want to add more elements or even more balloons.

SUPER CHALLENGE

Make a contraption that uses TWO of each of the six different simple machines (or even THREE!). Try to use different examples of each type of simple machine. For the wedge, for example, use a traditional doorstop-type wedge in addition to a wedge that splits things apart.

Chapter 8

GO BIG!

Now you know everything! You've learned about force, motion, and work. You can name all six simple machines. You know how simple machines help us do our work. And you know how to use these simple machines to engineer crazy contraptions.

You could say that when you use simple machines to make a contraption, you are actually building a **compound machine**. There are many examples of compound machines in this book. The wheelbarrow is one. It combines a lever with a wheel and axle. A shovel is another—it has both a lever and a wedge. The head of the shovel is the wedge and the long handle is the lever. A bicycle is a more complex example of a compound machine because it consists of three simple machines working together.

ESSENTIAL QUESTION

In what ways do simple machines work together as compound machines and improve people's lives?

Take a look at a bicycle. Can you find all three simple machines? The first is easy: wheels and axles. Obviously, there are two of these. Can you find two different examples of levers? Handbrakes are one set of levers. The pedals are another! There is even a third lever on bikes with a gear shift—the shifter is the lever. The third simple machine on a bicycle is the pulley system in the chain and the gears.

Other everyday examples of compound machines include scissors, a pencil sharpener, a bulldozer, a stapler, a crane, and a pizza cutter. Putting simple machines together in different ways and in different combinations creates all sorts of compound machines. The possibilities are endless.

Bicycles contain three simple machines.

principle: the basic way that something works.

time-lapse: a technique in photography in which a single photo is taken at certain time intervals to record action or changes that take place through time. When the photos are shown, it appears that the slow action is actually taking place quickly.

HOW COMPOUND MACHINES HELP YOU DO WORK

Compound machines depend on each simple machine in the device to serve a purpose for the device as a whole. As the simple machines work together, they make your work easier, just like any simple machine alone would. But remember what you've learned about work and force.

Life-Size *Mouse Trap* Game

A man named Mark Perez loved the *Mouse Trap* game as a kid. His interest in the game never went away. As an adult, he imagined a life-size version as a piece of art. He started his project in 1998 in an old boat barn. Mark worked at his job during the day, then on the mouse trap at night. In 2005, he completed the 20 sculptures needed. When they were connected, they formed a life-size version of the old, favorite game.

With the help of a few performers, Mark took his creation around the United States. It appeared at festivals, museums, and science centers. Mark acted as a circus ringleader, making the mouse trap more of a show than just an exhibit. At first, the show was simply for fun. Then, he began to include science lessons. As you've learned about Rube Goldberg machines, each step involves physics. Mark and his fellow performers explained energy and mechanical advantage to the crowds. They talked about the force of gravity at play. And they pointed out the various simple machines at work.

Despite the effort it took to assemble and disassemble the *Mouse Trap*, Mark loved it. He especially valued the opportunity to give people real-life examples of physics and scientific **principles** at play. "When you experience it and hear the clanging of the metal, it is different," says Mark. "We make it fun."

You can watch the *Mouse Trap* being built in this time-lapse video.

🔎 life-size mouse trap video

PS

The compound machine does not do the work for you while you sit back and relax—unless that machine has a motor connected to some form of electricity. You are still doing the same amount of work. The difference, as with all single simple machines, is that you have to use less force.

As you probably guessed, a compound machine has an even greater mechanical advantage than a simple machine alone. In fact, the compound machine gains not just the mechanical advantage of the two or more machines added together. Instead, it multiplies the advantage.

Consider a pair of scissors. It is made of two levers and two wedges (the thin cutting blade on the inside and the wider, dull edge on the outside). In this case, you get a mechanical advantage from the levers. And you gain a mechanical advantage from the wedges.

The total **MECHANICAL ADVANTAGE** is the advantage from the **LEVERS** multiplied by the advantage gained from the **WEDGES**.

With a bicycle, the advantage is that gained from the wheel and axle multiplied by that gained from the levers, multiplied again by the mechanical advantage of the pulley (the gears and chain). This might sound complicated. But remember, the end result is that a compound machine will make your work much easier than if you used a single simple machine.

The only exception to that is if your compound machine happens to be a Rube Goldberg machine! That's because sometimes it's just easier to do something in a straightforward way than in an overly complicated, Rube Goldberg kind of way. But obviously, building a contraption is far more fun.

Not only was Rube Goldberg a great inventor and cartoonist, he also predicted the future. His drawing called **"THE FUTURE OF HOME ENTERTAINMENT"** appeared on the March 15, 1967, cover of *Forbes* magazine. It featured a **family with each member (even the cat!) watching their own flat screen television and paying no** attention to one another.

Check out this video by the band OK Go. They made a Rube Goldberg contraption for the music video for the song, "This Too Shall Pass." It went viral and has received more than 50 million views.

🔎 OK Go Goldberg

In addition to learning about force, motion, work, and simple machines, you've also learned how everyday items in your home can be used to make crazy contraptions (or shall we call them compound machines?). Maybe now you see things in new ways and have an eye for stuff that could be used in a contraption. Have you found yourself saying, "No! Don't throw away that toilet paper roll!"? Maybe you've started a collection of milk bottle caps. You might have even found yourself fishing things out of the trash because they'd be useful.

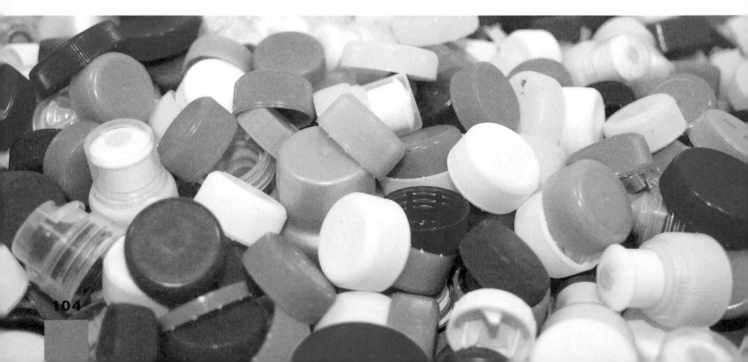

Above all, though, you've had fun and used your brain. You've learned to brainstorm and design and test and evaluate like an engineer. Next, you will find challenges that are bigger, smaller, and louder.

Maybe, even after turning the last page of this book, you will continue to build contraptions that are limited only by your imagination.

ESSENTIAL QUESTION

In what ways do simple machines work together as compound machines and improve people's lives?

Rube in the Movies

Almost from the start, Rube Goldberg's machines captured the interest of the public. They were also a source of inspiration in many movies. It started with a movie Goldberg wrote himself, *Soup to Nuts*, in 1930. The black-and-white comedy featured a crazy inventor who created such oddities as a self-tipping hat and a contraption to keep out burglars that included a giant mechanical boot, a large wooden mallet, and a cat. Silent film comedian Charlie Chaplin (1889–1977) also did a movie with a scene that involved a very Rube Goldberg-like automated feeding machine (*Modern Times*, 1936).

Later, in 1968, the movie *Chitty Chitty Bang Bang* featured a Rube Goldberg machine with only purpose—to make breakfast. Another Rube Goldberg breakfast-making machine appeared in *Pee-wee's Big Adventure* in 1985. That contraption involved fans, flames, a mini Ferris wheel, a flying toy dinosaur, and an automatic flapjack flipper. Also in 1985, *The Goonies* showed a contraption set up by kids to open a fence gate. Other movies that have some kind of contraption include *The Money Pit*, *Back to the Future* (the original and the third one), and *Ernest Goes to Jail*. Perhaps the most classic examples of Rube Goldberg's influence in movies are in *Home Alone* and *Home Alone 2*. In the movies, a young boy outwits a couple of would-be burglars with his creative traps and snares—some are simple devices while others involve more complicated chain reactions.

See Charlie Chaplin's automated feeding machine in action!

Chaplin eating machine

PS

GO
BIG

Okay, engineers, time to go big. Yes, you are going to make a contraption that is more life-sized than table-sized. If possible, make this contraption outside.

The Challenge Identified: Make an over-sized contraption, using each of the six simple machines, that will toss a ball to you.

Alert: Get permission from an adult to do this project.

❯ **Brainstorm ideas and supplies:** Think big. Start by considering where you will build this enormous thing—yard? Park? Basement? School? Also think about how you can use the biggest possible items in your contraption. For example, if you want dominoes, use cereal boxes instead of the normal-sized tiles. Or maybe blocks or boards. Marbles can be replaced with soccer balls. And instead of using small race cars, perhaps you have an old Big Wheel or a skateboard that can become part of a contraption. Slides on playgrounds make fun inclined planes. Maybe you even have one in your neighborhood that spirals like a screw! You get the idea.

National Geographic built a huge Rube Goldberg contraption as part of an advertising campaign. You should not use a person in a loop-de-loop, but ideally this will inspire you to go big.

🔎 Nat Geo contraption

Build a Life-Sized Catapult

If you want to have a huge catapult in your huge contraption, watch how these kids from Design Squad Global built theirs. After you build it, test it out. Consider what worked with your design and what didn't. What do you need to do to your large catapult to make it toss an object farther or more accurately? Then, consider how you can incorporate it into a large contraption.

🔎 PBS design squad

Draw a plan: It might look something like this.

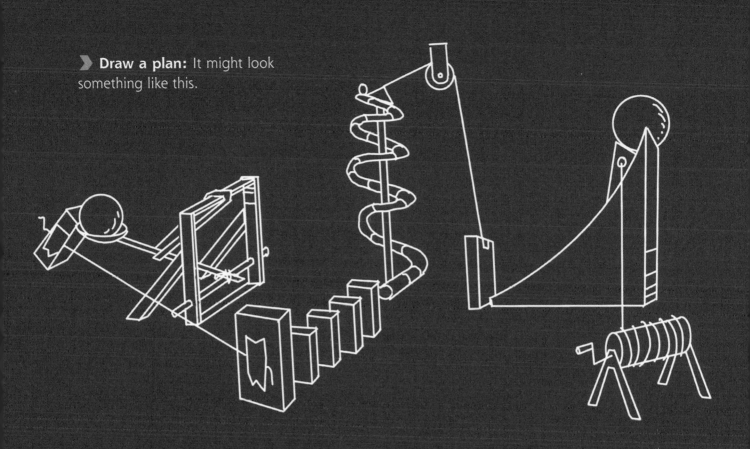

Build: Assemble all the parts of your over-sized contraption, set aside a good amount of time, and get ready to play ball.

Test: Get the motion started.

Evaluate: Was it fun building a huge contraption? Did it end up being easier or harder than you thought? How did all the elements work together? And, most importantly, did your contraption toss the ball to you? How were the forces you needed to apply different for this over-sized contraption than for the smaller ones?

Redesign? How could you do things differently the next time? Do you want to move elements around so they are at a different point in the chain reaction? While you were constructing, did you get ideas for other things you could include in a life-sized contraption? And maybe you want to add more elements.

GO SMALL

Now that you've gone big, it's time to go small. Save this one for a rainy day, maybe. In this challenge, you will make a teeny-tiny contraption.

The Challenge Identified: Make a miniature contraption that fits in a small box or case, using each of the six simple machines, to throw away a gum wrapper.

> **Brainstorm ideas and supplies:** Think small. Start by finding a shoebox or a small case you could use to build your contraption in. You may want to use toothpicks instead of popsicle sticks, or segments of a straw in place of toilet paper tubes. See if you can find small marbles or cars. What else can you find among your art supplies?

> **Draw a plan:** Here's one idea for a mini-contraption.

Contraption Hint: Because this challenge is to create a mini-contraption, you need to find mini-elements. One way to find what you need is to look through old toys to see if action figures, dolls, Legos, and others have accessories you can use in your design.

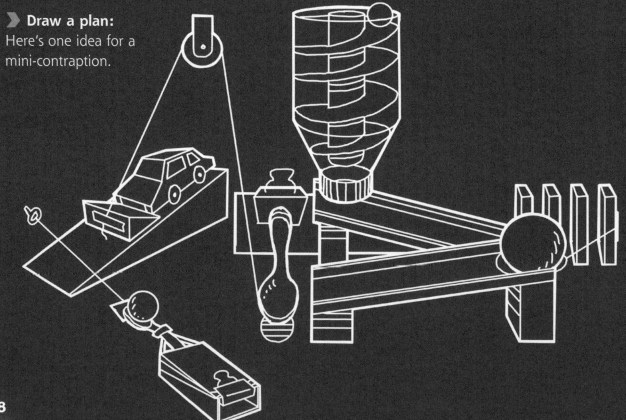

Melvin the Machine

A design studio in Holland created a miniature contraption that fit into two old suitcases. They named it Melvin the Magical Mixed Media Machine, or Melvin the Machine for short. The studio calls Melvin a Rube Goldberg machine with a twist. Not only does Melvin do what Rube Goldberg machines do, Melvin also has its own online identity. The first Melvin the studio built was big. **You can see it here.**

The second one they built, though, was designed to travel. Thus, it is small. **For ideas for your own mini-contraption, watch the video.** Your contraptions most likely won't be as delicate and intricate as this one, but it will ideally get you thinking. Take note of the different small materials used.

🔍 Melvin the Machine

🔍 Mini Melvin Machine

> **Build:** First, make sure all the parts of your contraption fit in the box or case when not put together. That's part of this challenge. Now, assemble your contraption. It can go beyond the borders of the box or case while set up.

> **Test:** Start the action and get that gum wrapper in the trash.

> **Evaluate:** What do you think about building a mini-contraption? Was it easier or harder than you thought? Did everyone else at home like that the mess was contained to one small box? Perhaps more importantly, did your contraption work as you wanted it to? Was it small but mighty? How were the forces you needed to apply in this contraption different from a normal-sized contraption?

The watch company, Seiko, developed a miniature Rube Goldberg contraption to use as an advertisement. **Check it out.**

🔍 Seiko Rube Goldberg

> **Redesign?** What other objects could you use in your mini-contraption to replace normal-sized items you've used for other challenges? Is there room in your box to make it more complex? To add elements?

GO
LOUD

For this last challenge you will go out with a bang. Literally.

The Challenge Identified: For this very last challenge, use each of the six simple machines to create a contraption of any size that makes **A LOT** of noise.

> **Alert:** Get permission from an adult to do this project.

❯ **Brainstorm ideas and supplies:** The most important elements in this contraption are the noisemakers. What will you use? A drum? Empty cans? A kazoo? A xylophone? All of the above? What other elements will you use?

❯ **Draw a plan:** Here's one possibility.

Build: Put it all together and warn the people nearby about the noise.

Test: Make some noise!

Evaluate: How much noise did you make? Was it enough? Do you need to make more? Or perhaps someone suggested you make less noise.

Redesign? What other noisemaker(s) could you use in your contraption? Could you make it bigger? Smaller? Can you put a noisemaker at each step of the chain reaction?

Super Challenge

Make a contraption that starts indoors, goes outdoors, and then back inside. Or, if the weather isn't cooperating, make a contraption that goes through two or three rooms of your home and back.

Final Challenge

Look back at your very first drawing—the one you drew before you even started building. You STILL aren't going to make a contraption that uses alligators or rockets or fire, but analyze that first drawing. Now that you know a lot more about force and motion and work, do you think that your first contraption could possibly perform as you want it to? What changes would you make? What additions would you make? Redraw that first sketch.

GLOSSARY

angle: the figure formed when two lines meet at the same point.

aqueduct: a pipe, channel, canal, or bridge built to carry water.

archaeologist: a scientist who studies ancient people through the objects they left behind.

Archimedes' screw: a machine used to raise water to a higher lever for irrigation. It consists of a screw inside a cylinder, and as the screw turns, it raises the water.

arm: the bar or plank of a lever that moves on a fulcrum.

arrowhead: the tip of an arrow. Native Americans crafted these tools from stone to help them hunt.

auger: a tool or device with a screw shaft that is used to make holes in wood, soil, ice, and other materials.

axis: the center, around which something rotates.

axle: the rod around which a wheel rotates.

backward design: the process of creating something starting with identifying what you want to accomplish, in order to determine the process needed to reach that goal.

balance scale: a device used for weighing things that balances weight on one side of the lever with what's being weighed on the other side.

BCE: put after a date, BCE stands for Before Common Era and counts down to zero. CE stands for Common Era and counts up from zero. These non-religious terms correspond to BC and AD. This book was printed in 2019 CE.

bloomers: old-fashioned loose pants for women and girls that are gathered at the knee or ankle.

bolt: a metal pin with screw threads. Used with a nut around the outside of the pin to hold things together.

brainstorm: to think creatively and without judgment, often in a group of people.

catapult: a device used to hurl or launch something.

chain reaction: a series of events in which one action causes the next one and so on.

chariot: an ancient, two-wheeled, horse-drawn cart used in parades and races.

chisel: a tool with a flat, sharpened edge used to cut, chip, or shape wood, stone, or metal.

compound machine: a machine that combines two or more simple machines to make work easier.

compound pulley: a pulley system that includes both a fixed and a moveable pulley.

contraption: a newfangled or complicated device.

conveyor belt: a system that uses a moving band of fabric, rubber, or metal to move objects easily; often seen in factories or in airports.

convoluted: complex and difficult to follow.

counterweight: a weight used to create a balance between it and something of equal weight.

cylinder: a solid figure with straight, parallel sides shaped into a circle or an oval, as in a can of soup or a paper towel roll.

device: a piece of equipment meant to do certain things, such as a phone.

efficient: work done with little waste of time or energy.

energy: the ability or power to do work or cause change.

engineer: someone who uses math, science, and creativity to solve problems and build things.

erosion: the gradual wearing away of rock or soil by water and wind.

exert: to put forth effort or force.

first class lever: a type of lever with the fulcrum in the middle, the load on one end, and the force applied on the other.

first law of motion: an object in motion will stay in motion (moving in the same direction at the same speed) unless some force acts on it. And an object at rest will stay at rest unless some force acts on it.

fixed pulley: a pulley system in which the pulley is fixed to a point and the rope is attached to the load or object.

force: a push or pull applied to an object that changes an object's motion.

friction: the force that slows a moving object or objects when they move against each other.

fulcrum: the fixed point on which a lever sits or is supported and on which it moves.

funnel: a cone that opens to a tube at the narrow end to direct downward flow.

gladiator: a warrior in ancient Rome who fought other gladiators or animals as a form of public entertainment.

grade: in physics, the amount of slope on an inclined plane.

gravity: a force that pulls objects toward each other and all objects to the earth.

groove: a line cut into a surface, often made in order to guide something such as rope along the rim of a wheel in a pulley system.

helix: a three-dimensional shape that winds evenly around a central axis.

improvise: to create with little preparation using materials easily obtained.

inclined plane: a flat surface with one end raised higher than the other.

Industrial Revolution: a period of time beginning in the late 1700s when people started using machines to make things in large factories.

irrigation: a system for bringing water through ditches to farmland.

kinetic energy: the energy of an object in motion.

knighted: given the title "Sir" by a British king or queen in recognition of one's achievements or service to his country.

legacy: something handed down from the past that has a long-lasting impact.

legend: an old story usually based on historical facts but that is not proven to be true.

lever: a simple machine made of a rigid bar that pivots on a support, called a fulcrum.

linear: of or having to do with a straight line.

load: something that is carried or moved, especially something heavy.

magnetism: the force that attracts or repels between magnets.

makeshift: using whatever is around as a temporary substitute.

mass: the measure of how much matter is in an object; the weight of an object in relation to its size.

matter: anything that has weight and takes up space. Almost everything is made of matter!

mechanical advantage: the benefit gained by using a machine to do work with less effort.

Mesopotamia: an ancient civilization located between the Tigris and Euphrates Rivers, in what is today part of Iraq.

mining: taking minerals, such as coal or gold, from the ground.

moveable pulley: a pulley system in which the load is attached directly to the pulley. One end of the rope is fixed to a point, and the other end of the rope can be free or fixed.

native: belonging to an area or region.

nonlinear: not in a straight line.

nut: a donut-shaped piece of metal with screw threads on the inner circle. Used with a bolt through the center to hold things together.

orbit: the path of an object circling another object in space.

output force: the amount of force exerted on an object by a simple machine.

patent: a legal document that gives an inventor the sole right to their invention so that others may not make, use, or sell the invention.

pegboard: a board with an evenly spaced pattern of small holes for pegs.

perpendicular: a line at a 90-degree angle, called a right angle, to another line, plane, or surface.

physicist: a scientist who studies physics.

physics: the study of physical forces, including matter, energy, and motion, and how these forces interact with each other.

pivot: to turn or move on a fixed spot.

plane: a flat or level surface.

potential energy: the stored energy of an object due to its state or position.

precise: exact, very accurate.

primates: a group of intelligent animals that includes humans, apes, and monkeys.

principle: the basic way that something works.

pulley: a simple machine consisting of a wheel with a grooved rim that a rope or chain is pulled through to help lift up a load.

rotate: to turn around a fixed point.

Rube Goldberg: a person whose name is used as an adjective. It describes accomplishing by complex means what seemingly could be done simply.

screw: a simple machine that has an inclined plane wrapped around a central axis. It is used to lift objects or hold things together.

screw press: a device that uses the mechanical advantage of a screw to apply force.

second class lever: a type of lever with the fulcrum at one end, the load in the middle, and the force applied at the other end.

second law of motion: a push or a pull on an object will change the speed of motion. The heavier an object is, the more force is needed to make that object speed up or slow down.

shaft: a long, narrow rod that forms the handle of a tool or club.

shears: a type of scissors with longer blades that are generally used for cutting heavy material.

simple machine: a tool that uses one movement to complete work.

slope: a plane with one end higher than the other.

snips: a type of hand-held shears used for cutting sheet metal.

steam engine: an engine powered by steam created by heating water.

STEM: an acronym that stands for science, technology, engineering, and mathematics. STEAM is STEM plus art.

superfluous: more than is necessary or wanted.

technology: the tools, methods, and systems used to solve a problem or do work.

terrace: a raised, flat platform or area of land.

theory: an unproven idea that explains why something is the way it is.

third class lever: a type of lever with the fulcrum at one end, the load on the other end, and the force applied in the middle.

third law of motion: for every action, there is an equal and opposite reaction.

threads: the inclined plane that wraps around the axis of the screw.

time-lapse: a technique in photography in which a single photo is taken at certain time intervals to record action or changes that take place through time. When the photos are shown, it appears that the slow action is actually taking place quickly.

trial and error: trying first one thing, then another and another, until something works.

watermill: a machine rotated by moving water to grind grain or do work. It converts the energy of the moving water to mechanical energy.

wedge: a simple machine that is thick at one end and narrows to a thin edge at the other. A wedge is used for splitting, tightening, and securing objects.

wheel and axle: a wheel with a rod that turn together to lift and move loads.

windmill: a machine rotated by wind to pump water or do work. It converts the energy of the wind to mechanical energy.

work: in physics, when a force acts on an object to move it some distance.

World's Fair: an international show to exhibit the achievements of countries from around the world and get a glimpse at the future.

Metric Conversions

Use this chart to find the metric equivalents to the English measurements in this book. If you need to know a half measurement, divide by two. If you need to know twice the measurement, multiply by two. How do you find a quarter measurement? How do you find three times the measurement?

English	Metric
1 inch	2.5 centimeters
1 foot	30.5 centimeters
1 yard	0.9 meter
1 mile	1.6 kilometers
1 pound	0.5 kilogram
1 teaspoon	5 milliliters
1 tablespoon	15 milliliters
1 cup	237 milliliters

BOOKS

Doudna, Kelly. *The Kids' Book of Simple Machines: Cool Projects & Activities that Make Science Fun!* Mighty Media Kids, 2015.

George, Jennifer, editor. *The Art of Rube Goldberg: (A) Inventive (B) Cartoon (C) Genius.* Abrams, 2013.

George, Jennifer. *Rube Goldberg's Simple Normal Humdrum School Day.* Abrams Books for Young Readers, 2017.

Yasuda, Anita. *Explore Simple Machines! With 25 Great Projects.* Nomad Press, 2011.

MUSEUMS

Exploratorium: exploratorium.edu

National Inventors Hall of Fame: invent.org

WEBSITES

Amazing Inventions, DK Find Out! dkfindout.com/us/science/amazing-inventions

Design Squad Global, PBS Kids pbskids.org/designsquad

Engineering for Kids, Science for Kids sciencekids.co.nz/engineering.html

Engineering: Simple Machines teachengineering.org/lessons/view/cub_simple_lesson01

Inductees, National Inventors Hall of Fame: invent.org/inductees

Rube Goldberg—The World of Hilarious Invention! rubegoldberg.com

RESOURCES

QR CODE GLOSSARY

RESOURCES

QR CODE GLOSSARY (CONTINUED)

page 78: youtube.com/watch?v=863z_eHGIJw

page 85: youtube.com/watch?time_continue=7&v=14N9Jlpjg1w

page 87: pbs.org/wnet/secrets/the-lost-gardens-of-babylon-video-archimedes-screw-the-date-tree-of-babylon/1169

page 91: youtube.com/watch?v=SEhI8NgwO8w

page 92: youtube.com/watch?v=82oepNoBKz0

page 93: teachengineering.org/activities/view/cmu_rube_activity1

page 95: slideserve.com/lynton/how-to-make-an-archimedes-screw

page 95: frugalfun4boys.com/simple-machines-lesson-lift-water-archimedes-screw

page 95: ymiclassroom.com/wp-content/uploads/2013/09/7wondersbabylon_act3.pdf

page 102: youtube.com/watch?time_continue=8&v=OQKN9kdWu6Q

page 104: youtube.com/watch?v=qybUFnY7Y8w

page 105: youtube.com/watch?time_continue=5&v=n_1apYo6-Ow

page 106: pbskids.org/designsquad/video/build-catapult

page 106: youtube.com/watch?v=Yw4IJXPTJXk

page 109: melvinthemachine.com/about

page 109: mini.melvinthemachine.com

page 109: youtube.com/watch?time_continue=3&v=tI-3jvMb-98

ESSENTIAL QUESTIONS

Introduction: What was Rube Goldberg's contribution to engineering?

Chapter 1: What roles do force, work, and energy play in Rube Goldberg contraptions?

Chapter 2: How do inclined planes help people do work and build Rube Goldberg contraptions?

Chapter 3: What role do levers play in today's world?

Chapter 4: How might history have been different without wheels?

Chapter 5: What are some inventions made possible by pulleys?

Chapter 6: How do wedges help people do work?

Chapter 7: How have screws been used throughout history to make work easier?

Chapter 8: In what ways do simple machines work together as compound machines and improve people's lives?

SUPPLIES YOU'LL FIND HANDY

Top 5 Handy Supplies

Glue gun
(and glue sticks!)

Tape

Dominoes

Empty TP rolls

Popsicle sticks

Toys

Marbles

Balls

Tennis ball

Softball

Baseball

Bowling balls

Toy cars

Car tracks

Skateboard

Roller skates

Golf balls

Ping pong balls

Toy trains

Wooden blocks

Legos

Toy trains

Toy train tracks

Marble runs

Action figures

Stuffed animals

Art Supplies

Graph paper

String

Yarn

Rubber bands

Tape

Pins

Pencils

Binder clips

Scissors

Recyclables

Cereal boxes

Plastic water bottles

Plastic bottle caps

Cans

Aluminum foil

Plastic containers

Cardboard

Toilet paper and paper
towel rolls

Lids

Miscellaneous

Clothespins

Chopsticks

Straws

Toothpicks

Bowls

Hammer

Balloons

Funnel

Bucket

Cups and bowls

Straws

Trays

Pieces of wood

PVC pipe

Plastic tubing

Gutters

Plastic spoons

Rope

Pulley

Peg board

Thread spools

Ribbon spools

POSSIBLE TASKS OR CHALLENGES

Knock something over

Ring a bell

Pop a balloon

Open/close a door

Raise a flag

Open/shut a window

Pull curtains open/closed

Roll a dice

Swat a fly

Trap a leprechaun

Stamp an envelope

Rattle a wind chime

Turn on/off a light

Hit an easy button

Knock a bone off a table for the dog

Launch a dog treat

Water a plant

Plant seeds in a pot

Destroy a house of cards

Squeeze toothpaste onto a brush

Close a book

Turn a page in a book

Toss a gum wrapper in the trash

Play with the cat

Deliver a note

Deliver a cookie or candy

Zip a zipper

Bother a sibling

Play with the cat

Apply a bandage

Wake up the dog

Dispense a drop of soap

Bang a drum

Open an umbrella

Make tea/dunk a tea bag

Turn on a CD player

Display a message/memo

Get a marble/ball in a goal/bucket

Launch a basketball through a hoop

Trap a mouse

Put a stamp on a letter

Trap a toy monster

Turn on/off a fan

Sail a boat across a "pond"

Screw in a light bulb

Tighten the lid on a jar or bottle

Staple papers together

Raise a flag

Feed the dog (or cat or hamster or whatever you have!)

Turn on/off a water faucet

Erase a chalkboard

Put coins in a piggy bank

Pour a bowl of cereal

Bowl a strike

Drop a coin in a piggy bank

INDEX

INDEX

force
  definition of, 6, 17
  friction as, 18, 51, 54, 65
  gravity as, iv, 6, 14, 17–18, 19, 27, 51,
    65, 88, 102
  inclined planes and, 27–28
  laws of motion and, 13–16, 23
  levers and, 36–39, 41–42
  pulleys and, 65, 67
  screws and, 88, 90–91
  wedges and, 78–79
  wheels, axles, and, 48, 51–52, 54
  work, energy, and, 19–21, 102–103
friction, 18, 51, 54, 65
fulcrum, 36–39, 44, 46, 77
funnels, 93

G

general relativity, theory of, 17
Goldberg, Reuben "Rube," v, 2–7, 105. *See
  also* Rube Goldberg contraptions
Grand Central Terminal, 27
gravity, iv, 6, 14, 17–18, 19, 27, 51, 65, 88,
  102
Guggenheim Museum, 28

H

hammer claws, 40, 41
Handler, Ruth and Elliot, 51
Hanging Gardens of Babylon, 87
hinges, 42
Hot Wheels cars, v, 51, 52

I

inclined planes, iv, 21, 25–35. *See also*
  screws

K

kinetic energy, 19–20
kinetic sculptures, 97

L

levers, iv–v, 6, 21, 36–47, 50, 77, 92,
  100–101, 103
lids, v, 90, 93, 96–97
light bulbs, 53, 90, 93
load, 37–38, 63–66, 86

M

Mason, John Landis, v, 90
mass, 14–15, 17, 23
mechanical advantage, iv, 22, 28, 41, 52,
  61, 65, 78–79, 90–91, 102–103
Melvin the Machine, 109
Michelangelo, 76
motion, laws of, iv, 13–16, 23–24
Mouse Trap, 8, 92, 102
moveable pulleys, 63–64, 65–67, 70–71
movies, contraptions in, 105

N

nails, 40, 41, 75, 79
Newton, Isaac, iv, 13–14, 17–18, 24. *See
  also* motion, laws of

O

output force, 78, 91

P

patents, 40, 66
Perez, Mark, 102
physics, 6, 12–21, 23–24, 102
potential energy, 19–20
pottery wheels, 49
pulleys, iv–v, 6, 21, 60–73, 101, 103
pull/push, 15, 17–18, 19
pyramids, iv, 26–27, 34–35

INDEX